# Famous People of China

## The History and Culture of China

Mason Crest Publishers   Philadelphia

Yan Liao

# Famous People of China

The History and Culture of China

Mason Crest Publishers   Philadelphia

Yan Liao

Produced by OTTN Publishing, Stockton, New Jersey

**Mason Crest Publishers**
370 Reed Road
Broomall, PA 19008
www.masoncrest.com

First printing

1 3 5 7 9 8 6 4 2

Library of Congress Cataloging-in-Publication Data

Liao, Yan.
   Famous people of China / Yan Liao.
      p. cm. — (China)
   Audience: Age 12.
   Audience: Grades 7-8.
   Includes bibliographical references and index.
   ISBN 1-59084-826-8
   1. China—Biography—Juvenile literature. I. Title. II. Series.
   DS734.L5154 2004
   920.051— dc22

                          2004019891

# Table of Contents

# Introduction

**Dr. Jianwei Wang**
**University of Wisconsin–**
**Stevens Point**

Before his first official visit to the United States in December 2003, Chinese premier Wen Jiabao granted a lengthy interview to the *Washington Post*. In that interview, he observed: "If I can speak very honestly and in a straightforward manner, I would say the understanding of China by some Americans is not as good as the Chinese people's understanding of the United States." Needless to say, Mr. Wen is making a sweeping generalization here. From my personal experience and observation, some Americans understand China at least as well as some Chinese understand the United States. But overall there is some truth in Mr. Wen's remarks. For example, if you visited a typical high school in China, you would probably find that students there know more about the United States than their American counterparts know about China. For one thing, most Chinese teenagers start learning English in high school, while only a very small fraction of American high school students will learn Chinese.

In a sense, the knowledge gap between Americans and Chinese about each other is understandable. For the

Chinese, the United States is the most important foreign country, representing not just the most developed economy, unrivaled military might, and the most advanced science and technology, but also a very attractive political and value system, which many Chinese admire. But for Americans, China is merely one of many foreign countries. As citizens of the world's sole superpower, Americans naturally feel less compelled to learn from others. The Communist nature of the Chinese polity also gives many Americans pause. This gap of interest in and motivation to learn about the other side could be easily detected by the mere fact that every year tens of thousands of Chinese young men and women apply for a visa to study in the United States. Many of them decide to stay in this country. In comparison, many fewer Americans want to study in China, let alone live in that remote land.

Nevertheless, for better or worse, China is becoming more and more important to the United States, not just politically and economically, but also culturally. Most notably, the size of the Chinese population in the United States has increased steadily. China-made goods as well as Chinese food have become a part of most Americans' daily life. China is now the third-largest trade partner of the United States and will be a huge market for American goods and services. China is also one of the largest creditors, with about $100 billion in U.S. government securities. Internationally China could either help or hinder American foreign policy in the United Nations, on issues ranging from North Korea to non-proliferation of weapons of mass destruction. In the last century, misperception of this vast country cost the United States dearly in the Korean War and the Vietnam War. On the issue of Taiwan, China and the United States may once again embark on a collision course if both sides are not careful in handling the dispute. Simply put, the state of U.S.-China relations may well shape the future not just for Americans and Chinese, but for the world at large as well.

The main purpose of this series, therefore, is to help high school students form an accurate, comprehensive, and balanced understanding of China, past and present, good and bad, success and failure, potential and limit, and culture and state. At least three major images will emerge from various volumes in this series.

First is the image of traditional China. China has the longest continuous civilization in the world. Thousands of years of history produced a rich and sophisticated cultural heritage that still influences today's China. While this ancient civilization is admired and appreciated by many Chinese as well as foreigners, it can also be heavy baggage that makes progress in China difficult and often very costly. This could partially explain why China, once the most advanced country in the world, fell behind during modern times. Foreign encroachment and domestic trouble often plunged this ancient nation into turmoil and war. National rejuvenation and restoration of the historical greatness is still considered the most important mission for the Chinese people today.

Second is the image of Mao's China. The establishment of the People's Republic of China in 1949 marked a new era in this war-torn land. Initially the Communist regime was quite popular and achieved significant accomplishments by bringing order and stability back to Chinese society. When Mao declared that the "Chinese people stood up" at Tiananmen Square, "the sick man of East Asia" indeed reemerged on the world stage as a united and independent power. Unfortunately, Mao soon plunged the country into endless political campaigns that climaxed in the disastrous Cultural Revolution. China slipped further into political suppression, diplomatic isolation, economic backwardness, and cultural stagnation.

Third is the image of China under reform. Mao's era came to an abrupt end after his death in 1976. Guided by Deng Xiaoping's farsighted and courageous policy of reform and openness, China has experienced earth-shaking changes in the last quarter century. With the adoption of a market economy, China has transformed itself into a global economic powerhouse in only two decades. China has also become a full-fledged member of the international community, as exemplified by its return to the United Nations and its accession to the World Trade Organization. Although China is far from being democratic as measured by Western standards, overall it is now a more humane place to live, and the Chinese people have begun to enjoy unprecedented freedom in a wide range of social domains.

These three images of China, strikingly different, are closely related with one another. A more sophisticated and balanced perception of China needs to take into consideration all three images and the process of their evolution from one to another, thus acknowledging the great progress China has made while being fully aware that it still has a long way to go. In my daily contact with Americans, I quite often find that their views of China are based on the image of traditional China and of China under Mao—they either discount or are unaware of the dramatic changes that have taken place. Hopefully this series will allow its readers to observe the following realities about China.

First, China is not black and white, but rather—like the United States—complex and full of contradictions. For such a vast country, one or two negative stories in the media often do not represent the whole picture. Surely the economic reforms have reduced many old problems, but they have also created many new problems. Not all of these problems, however, necessarily prove the guilt of the Communist system. Rather, they may be the result of the very reforms the government has been implementing and of the painful transition from one system to another. Those who would view China through a single lens will never fully grasp the complexity of that country.

Second, China is not static. Changes are taking place in China every day. Anyone who lived through Mao's period can attest to how big the changes have been. Every time I return to China, I discover something new. Some things have changed for the better, others for the worse. The point I want to make is that today's China is a very dynamic society. But the development in China has its own pace and logic. The momentum of changes comes largely from within rather than from without. Americans can facilitate but not dictate such changes.

Third, China is neither a paradise nor a hell. Economically China is still a developing country with a very low per capita GDP because of its huge population. As the Chinese premier put it, China may take another 100 years to catch up with the United States. China's political system remains authoritarian and can be repressive and arbitrary. Chinese people still do not have as much freedom as American people enjoy, particularly when it comes to expressing opposition to the government. So China is certainly not an ideal society, as its leaders used to believe (or at least declare). Yet the Chinese people as a whole are much better off today than they were 20 years ago, both economically and politically. Chinese authorities were fond of telling the Chinese people that Americans lived in an abyss of misery. Now every Chinese knows that this is nonsense. It is equally ridiculous to think of the Chinese in a similar way.

Finally, China is both different from and similar to the United States. It is true that the two countries differ greatly in terms of political and social systems and cultural tradition. But it is also true that China's program of reform and openness has made these two societies much more similar. China is largely imitating the United States in many aspects. One can easily detect the convergence of the two societies in terms of popular culture, values, and lifestyle by walking on the streets of Chinese cities like Shanghai. With ever-growing economic and other functional interactions, the two countries have also become increasingly interdependent. That said, it is naïve to expect that China will become another United States. Even if China becomes a democracy one day, these two great nations may still not see eye to eye on many issues.

Understanding an ancient civilization and a gigantic country such as China is always a challenge. If this series kindles readers' interest in China and provides them with systematic information and thoughtful perspectives, thus assisting their formation of an informed and realistic image of this fascinating country, I am sure the authors of this series will feel much rewarded.

The Temple of Heaven in Beijing was built as a place for China's emperors to offer prayers and sacrifices to the gods. Two emperors are among the fascinating and noteworthy figures profiled in this book.

# Overview

In his poem "Memories of the Past at Red Cliff," Su Dongpo wrote: "To match the hills and the rivers so fair, / How many heroes of yore / Made a great show!" Looking back at China's past, we can't help but feel the same today as this great poet from a thousand years ago.

China is one of the four oldest civilizations in the world; its history extends back more than 5,000 years. Over the centuries, innumerable Chinese have distinguished themselves in all fields of endeavor, in the process shaping the development of their nation and its remarkable culture.

In a short volume such as this, it would be impossible even to mention all the people who have made outstanding contributions to Chinese life, much less to describe their accomplishments in detail. Rather, this book seeks to introduce a handful of prominent figures who not only shone in various fields but also lived at different periods in China's long history, from pre-dynastic times to the late 20th century. It is hoped that the brief profiles offered here might spark readers to further explorations of Chinese history and culture.

## Who Is Included

The first famous person presented in this book (which is organized chronologically) is also arguably the single most important figure in Chinese civilization. Indeed, very few persons in the course of human history have influenced a nation more profoundly than the philosopher Confucius has influenced China. Although this great sage of ancient times left little written work—mostly a collection of his sayings, compiled by students after his death—his teachings shaped governance and social relations in China for two millennia, and their effect on the Chinese world of today can hardly be overstated. Confucianism centers on *ren* (*jen* in the system formerly used to transliterate Chinese characters), a love for our fellow beings; it advocates that individuals change society by first cultivating their own virtue and then placing their families in order.

Despite Confucianism's singular importance, it should be noted that Chinese civilization has other philosophical foundations. Taoism, traditionally said to have been formulated by a contemporary of Confucius called Laozi (Lao-tzu) and later by

**This bronze sculpture, made during the Song dynasty (960–1279), depicts the Chinese philosopher Laozi (Lao-tzu) riding a water buffalo. As a founder of Taoism, Laozi is an important figure in Chinese history.**

Zhuangzi (Chuang-tzu), was another leading school of thought for the Chinese. It is characterized by a deep love of nature, a simple lifestyle free of material striving, and a disavowal of rigid social conventions and rules. Most Chinese are Taoist in private and Confucian in public. Thus, to understand the Chinese mind, one must study both of these philosophies.

Many Chinese kings and emperors have won long-lasting fame for their achievements as rulers of one of the most advanced and powerful nations in the world. Emperor Wudi (Wu-ti) of the Han dynasty, Emperor Taizong (T'ai-tsung) of the Tang dynasty, and Emperor Kangxi (K'ang-hsi) and Emperor Qianlong (Ch'ien-lung) of the Qing (Ch'ing) dynasty are but a few such figures, each of whom could easily be the subject of a full-length biography. This book, however, examines the life and legacy of another famous Chinese emperor: Qin Shihuang (Ch'in Shih-huang). In the third century B.C., he established the first unified empire of China and set up a centralized government that was the model for all Chinese dynasties in the centuries to follow. Qin Shihuang standardized the writing system, currency, and measures, and he built the Great Wall of China, the country's most enduring symbol. He was also a ruthless tyrant. Yet his influence on Chinese history was far-reaching, which justifies his inclusion in this volume.

In China, as in most cultures throughout the world, women have often been relegated to subordinate roles. Yet over the years, many exceptional females have risen to prominence in Chinese political and cultural life. Wu Zetian (Wu Tse-t'ien), who is profiled in this book, became the only woman in China's long history to rule the country in her own right. Although frequently maligned for the ruthlessness with which she pursued power, Wu Zetian proved a very competent ruler who led China into one of its most prosperous times.

China has produced many outstanding literary talents. Some people might argue for Li Bai (Li Pai), the great romantic poet

**Dr. Sun Yat-sen (1866–1925) addresses an audience at his home in Guilin, in the province of Guangxi, circa 1922. After leading a revolution that overthrew China's last emperor, Sun in 1912 became provisional president of the short-lived Chinese republic.**

from the Tang dynasty, as China's finest poet. However, Su Dongpo (Su Tung-p'o), who lived later during the Song (Sung) dynasty, was Li Bai's equal in literary ability, and his poetry displays more versatility. A favorite of poetry-loving Chinese to this day, Su Dongpo is profiled in this volume.

Two famous persons in this book lived during the Ming dynasty. One is an explorer named Zheng He (Cheng Ho), who led seven grand ocean expeditions into the Indian Ocean, the Persian Gulf, and the Red Sea, reaching as far as East Africa. These expeditions, more than 50 years earlier than the great voyages of the Portuguese and the Spanish at the end of the 15th century, assembled the world's largest fleet and spread the Chinese culture across Southeast Asia. The other Ming Chinese is Li Shizhen (Li Shih-chen), one of the most famous doctors in traditional Chinese medicine, who compiled a monumental reference work on Chinese pharmacology.

Contemporary China has been shaped by a number of persons who helped bring their lagging country into the modern world. Scholars in the late 19th century such as Kang Youwei (K'ang Yu-wei) and Liang Qichao (Liang Ch'i-ch'ao) promoted new ideas from the West and paved the way for China's great changes in the following hundred years. And then Sun Yat-sen, a doctor-turned-revolutionist, led the revolution of 1911–1912, which overthrew the Qing, China's last feudal dynasty, and established the first republic in this ancient land. Yet no one has had a more profound effect on modern China than Mao Zedong, the last famous person examined in this book. Mao led his country through a Communist revolution and in 1949 founded the People's Republic of China, which he ruled—for good and ill—for more than 25 years. Although his successors have charted a somewhat different course, particularly in the economic realm, Mao's legacy continues to loom large.

This 19th-century Chinese illustration depicts Confucius (or more accurately, Kongzi), the philosopher whose teachings became the basis of Chinese social and political life for more than 2,000 years.

# The Great Sage

More than 2,500 years have passed since Kongzi (K'ung-tzu)—or Confucius as he is better known in the West—walked the dusty roads of China. But the influence of this great philosopher and educator is still felt in every corner of the country, as well as in many other East Asian and Southeast Asian nations. Although not a religious leader, Confucius has attained a status like that of Muhammad in the Muslim world or Jesus in the Western cultures: for more than two millennia, his thought and teaching have defined the Chinese character and today remain an inseparable part of the culture.

## A Lifetime of Learning and Teaching

According to legend, signs portended greatness for Confucius even before his birth, when his mother was visited by a *qilin* (*ch'i lin*), the Chinese unicorn. The unicorn spit out a tablet of precious stone upon which was written, "The son of the essence of water will succeed the weak Zhou dynasty and become an uncrowned king." Confucius's mother marveled at this sign and tied a red ribbon on the unicorn. A few days later, she went up a nearby mountain to pray for a boy. She was granted the wish. At Confucius's birth, the legend goes, two dragons came down from the clouds and encircled the house, and five old men descended to the yard.

The actual circumstances of Confucius's birth were no doubt more mundane, and in his early years he knew hardship. He was born into the Kong (K'ung) family in 551 B.C., near Qufu (Ch'u-fu), the capital city of the small feudal state of Lu, located in present-day Shandong (Shan-tung) Province between Beijing and Shanghai. Records suggest that his father was of noble ancestry, but by the time Confucius came into the world, his family had declined. Confucius's father died when he was three, and thereafter he and his mother lived in poverty.

It is not clear what kind of education Confucius received—he seems to have been mostly self-taught—but from a young age he developed a love of books and learning. "At fifteen," he says in *Lun Yu* (*The Analects*), "I set my heart on learning." Eventually he became the most learned man of his time.

At age 19, Confucius secured a job managing a provincial granary. This was a duty of great importance, for grains at that time were used as money. Later he supervised a grazing land and kept track of oxen and sheep. He was said to have always kept good records.

Confucius married at 19, and he and his wife eventually had one son and one daughter. The historical records contain little information about Confucius's wife, which is not surprising, as Chinese women usually led a submissive life.

When Confucius was 24, his mother died. He observed a three-year-long mourning period for her.

**The marker outside this cave in the Ni Mountains near Qufu indicates that it was the birthplace of Confucius.**

During these years, Confucius devoted himself to the study of history, philosophy, and literature. Among the ancient texts he studied were *Shu Jing* (*Shu Ching*), the *Book of History,* an account of the words and deeds of the old hero-kings; and *Shi Jing* (*Shih Ching*), the *Book of Poems*, a collection of ancient songs and poems. He also became well acquainted with rituals and ceremonies from close studies of the ancient rites and sacrificial ceremonies.

By the age of 30, Confucius had developed a systematic way of thinking and had become a famous teacher, attracting students from near and far. Before Confucius, scholarship and teaching were mostly leisure activities of aristocrats and officials, and education was reserved for the ruling class. Confucius was the first Chinese to make teaching a profession and extend education to commoners. He put forth the idea that education should be open to all, regardless of status and wealth, so that every young man of ability might have the opportunity to advance himself and serve as a leader. He welcomed students of all backgrounds, asking only for intelligence and an eagerness to learn.

Confucius believed that the purpose of education was for a person to cultivate morality as well as to gain knowledge so that he could become a government official and introduce reforms that would help bring good to the world. Therefore, Confucius taught his students not only history, literature, and philosophy, but also the ways of government. Like other ancient philosophers such as Plato, Confucius taught his students by way of discussions and debates, as is obvious in *The Analects*, a book that records his teaching and philosophy. Confucius was said to have had 3,000 students, among whom 72 achieved great scholarship. Although today the content of his teaching might seem dated, Confucius's fundamental principles of learning and teaching still hold great truth, as is reflected in his sayings, such as "Learning without thinking is pointless. Thinking without learning is precarious."

Confucius lived during the Spring and Autumn period (770 B.C.–476 B.C.). This was a time when China lacked strong central authority; the

**Confucius was the first Chinese thinker to champion the idea that education should be open to all males, not just members of the ruling class. This illustration, from a French book published in the early 20th century, depicts the great sage with some of his pupils. Confucius is believed to have taught 3,000 students over the course of his lifetime.**

ruling Zhou (Chou) dynasty, established in the 11th century B.C., had been forced by barbarian tribes to move its capital east from Xi'an (Hsi-an) to Luoyang (Lo-yang), after which its power had steadily eroded. Although the Zhou kings continued as China's rulers in name, in reality they had direct control only of the small area around the capital. Actual power belonged to the lords of the various feudal states that had arisen within the Zhou kingdom. These rulers fought one another constantly to expand their states and, ultimately, to gain supremacy over all of China. In order to support the endless warfare, as well as their lavish style of living, the feudal lords taxed their subjects heavily. In this environment, life for the common people was difficult at best.

The troubled times gave rise to a profusion of theories about government and human existence. Philosophers representing various schools of thought traveled from one state to another, offering their services to the feudal lords; these learned men could provide guidance and advice on political, military, and moral matters. Rulers eager to gain any possible advantage over their neighbor states embraced those schools of thought that they perceived as most useful and awarded their advocates high positions and ranks. For a few hundred years, the traveling consultants spread their philosophies across the vast land of China. This period, later called the Hundred Schools of Thought, is regarded as the golden age of Chinese philosophy.

Confucianism, the teaching and philosophy established by Confucius, was one of the four major philosophies of this period (the other three were Taoism, Legalism, and Mohism). Confucius believed he was living in a time during which China's ancient civilization had collapsed, and he looked to the remote past as a golden age. His basic philosophy on government is that the state should exist for the benefit and welfare of all people, and a ruler should govern not by force, but by establishing a moral example for his people. Confucius further declared that the right to govern should not depend on one's birth, but on his character and ability. In other words, the aristocrats who controlled the government during Confucius's day were not necessarily the rightful rulers, and commoners should be trusted with the power to govern if they had the ability and virtue.

Confucius was not content simply being a teacher; his ambition was to put his ideas into practice. He wanted to influence the rulers with his philosophy of government, to end the sufferings of the people, and to bring harmony to the world. In 497 B.C., when he was well into his fifties, he set out with a group of students on a journey as a traveling consultant. Hoping to convince some feudal lord to adopt his philosophy of government, he and his students traveled from one state to another, meeting with dukes and princes to discuss his ideas. However, Confucius refused to flatter those in power, and his philosophy of government set such high standards that most feudal lords found them threatening rather than practical. In 484 B.C., after 13 long and fruitless years, Confucius returned to his home state of Lu, where he devoted the rest of his life to teaching and studying.

Confucius's last years were saddened by the death of his only son and his favorite student Yan Hui (Yen Hui), whom he had thought would be the heir of his philosophy. The great sage himself died in 479 B.C. and was buried on the riverbank north of Qufu.

## The Confucian Way

The enduring importance of Confucius lies not in his life, but in his teaching and thought. During his final years, Confucius might have considered himself a failure, as he had never managed to secure an important government position or convert any ruler to his philosophy. After his death, however, his ideas were spread and further developed by his many followers. His conversations with his students were compiled into *The Analects*, which became the single most important book for Chinese scholars in the next 2,000 years.

Contrary to popular belief, Confucius was not a religious leader, nor is Confucianism a religion. Confucius was, as a matter of fact, a non-spiritual philosopher who was concerned primarily with personal and political morality and conduct. He very rarely mentioned the name of gods, and he frequently refused to discuss questions of immortality. When asked about spiritual beings, he remarked, "If we do not even know life, how can we know death?" Confucianism is a human-centered philosophy that deals mainly with common questions of life: how a person should live,

This inscribed stone pillar, or stela, marks the burial mound at the tomb of Confucius in Shandong Province.

what goals the person should strive to achieve, and how the person is related to fellow human beings.

Confucius believed in five primary human virtues: *ren* (*jen*), or benevolence; *yi* (*i*), or justice; *li*, or proper conduct; *zhi* (*chih*), or wisdom; and *xin* (*hsin*), or sincerity. The two most important of these virtues are *ren*, which can be understood as "a compassionate love for our fellow men," and *li*, which describes a combination of manners, ritual, custom, and etiquette. Individuals should cultivate

Because of a bump on his forehead, Confucius was given the name Qiu (Ch'iu), meaning "hill"; his literary name was Zhongni (Chung-ni). However, these two names were very seldom used, as it was a Chinese tradition to avoid referring to a person of status by his given names. Rather, the sage was called Kongfuzi (K'ung-fu-tzu), which means "Master Kong." When Jesuit missionaries first visited China in the 16th century and discovered this great philosopher, they Latinized "Kongfuzi" as "Confucius," by which he has always been known in the West.

the five primary virtues by way of education and constant reflection on their thoughts and behaviors. While the title *junzi* (*chün tzu*) literally meant "a prince's son" during his time, Confucius transformed it into a term for anybody who had cultivated the five virtues and thereby achieved an exemplary status. Ever since Confucius's time, *junzi*, which is roughly equivalent to "gentleman" in English, has become the highest state of personal development any Chinese man can hope to achieve.

Confucius stressed the family as the basic unit of society: a wholesome society, in his view, is based on harmonious families. The relationship between the governing and the governed, according to Confucius, resembles the relationship between parents and children. As parents should act with benevolence and children should obey and respect their parents, rulers should govern virtuously and subjects should be obedient to their rulers.

To change society for the better, individuals must first cultivate their own virtue and then place their families in order. In the Confucian view, a highly hierarchical structure characterizes all proper family and social relations. Sons should obey their fathers, and wives should follow the lead of their husbands. Younger friends should be subordinate to older friends. Ancestor worship, which was already a common religion prior to Confucius's time, was reinforced by his emphasis on family loyalty and respect for one's parents and elders. The concept of *xiao* (*hsiao*), or filial piety, extends also to deceased family ancestors, and this has since been one of the distinctive features of Chinese culture.

Although Confucius often said that he was merely passing on the wisdom and knowledge of the past, his philosophy was innovative in many ways. First of all, he popularized education, which had previously been reserved only for the rich and aristocratic. Furthermore, at a time of hereditary rulers, he argued that states should be governed by those with outstanding qualifications, regardless of their background. The state, Confucius said, exists for the welfare of its people; rulers, though given the "mandate of heaven" to govern, should cultivate personal virtue and present a shining example for their people.

Decades after Confucius's death, one of his followers, Mengzi (Meng-tzu), or Mencius, expanded on his philosophy of government. Mengzi put forth the theory that when rulers become tyrannical, they no longer hold the mandate of heaven, and in such cases, people have the right—or even the duty—to rebel against them and set up a new government. Over the following centuries, this theory became the justification for countless revolutions and dynastic changes in China.

## The Uncrowned King

Although Confucius died relatively unknown, his students—some of whom obtained high official posts—spread his philosophy widely,

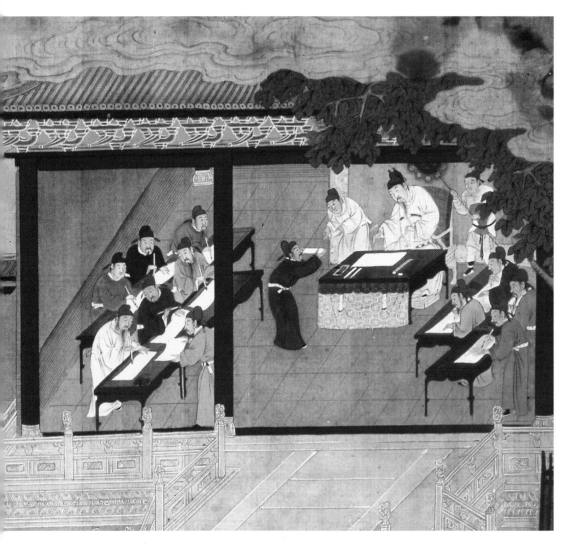

Centuries after Confucius's death, his ideas about governance were adopted by China's emperors, beginning with the Han dynasty (206 B.C.–A.D. 220). One practice inspired by the great sage was the use of civil service examinations—based largely on the Confucian classics—to select the most capable men for government posts. This watercolor on silk depicts Chinese men taking such a test during the Song dynasty.

and Confucianism became one of the major philosophies of the Hundred Schools of Thought. However, Confucianism suffered a major setback when China was united in 221 B.C. by the Qin (Ch'in) state. Qin rulers had long followed an opposing philosophy, Legalism, which emphasized the need for harsh laws and justified the absolute power of the ruler. Confucianism, with its emphasis on an educated public and virtuous rulers, was viewed as a threat by China's new Qin emperor. To eliminate its influence, he had all Confucian texts burned and several hundred Confucian scholars buried alive. However, the Qin dynasty lasted only 15 years before its harsh policies brought about its downfall. The succeeding Han dynasty (206 B.C.–A.D. 220) embraced Confucianism wholeheartedly and established it as its official state philosophy, which marked the beginning of the Confucian era in China.

Inspired by Confucian ideas of governance, Chinese emperors, starting with the Han dynasty, gradually developed the practice of selecting government officials by way of civil service examinations. These examinations, which were open to all, aimed at selecting the most knowledgeable and capable men for public service. In time, they developed into an examination system based primarily on the Confucian classics, which include *The Analects* and a few ancient works that Confucius had commented on, such as the *Book of History*. Because the examination system provided the only channel by which members of the lower class might advance to power, many thousands devoted years to the intensive study of the Confucian classics.

From the second century B.C. to the beginning of the 20th century—with occasional breakdowns and varying degrees of emphasis—Confucian thought served as the official ideology of all dynasties that ruled China, and Confucius himself was elevated to the status of a demigod. A Confucian temple could be found in every town or village, emperors held grand memorial ceremonies on the great sage's birthday, and in every school students and teachers bowed to his portrait in reverence. His descendants were treated like royalty in every dynasty, and today a clear family line can still be traced all the way back to the philosopher, which is a rarity even in China. Confucius might have died thinking himself a failure; little did he

# Confucius Said:

"Learning coupled with practice whenever possible—is it not joyful? Having a friend visiting from afar—is it not delightful? Harboring no displeasure for being not recognized—is it not gentlemanly?"

"Review the past to understand the future. Past is Teacher."

"Differentiate not those who seek to be taught."

"Worry not that people do not know you. Worry that you have not the ability."

"A gentleman is slow with words and quick with actions."

"A gentleman eats without expecting satiation, lives without expecting luxury, and is diligent in work and careful with words—these are steps to the right Direction. Such a person is a student of learning."

"I have yet to meet a person who is more interested in virtue than in beauty."

From *The Analects of Confucius: A New-Millennium Translation.*
Translated and annotated by David H. Li. Bethesda, Md.: Premier
Publishing Company, 1999.

know that he was to become the uncrowned king of China for more than 2,000 years.

In time, Confucianism spread to Japan, Korea, and some Southeast Asian countries such as Vietnam. It has greatly influenced all these cultures.

Today, Confucianism continues to define the fundamental values and shape the thought of Chinese people all around the world. For the Chinese, families, rather than individuals, remain the essential units of the society, and respect for education is nearly universal. Many of Confucius's remarks, beginning with "Confucius said," have entered the everyday language of the Chinese. Each year on his birthday, impressive ceremonies are held in his hometown of Qufu, as well as in many overseas Chinese communities, to celebrate this great sage, whose teaching and thought are inseparable from the Chinese identity as we know it today.

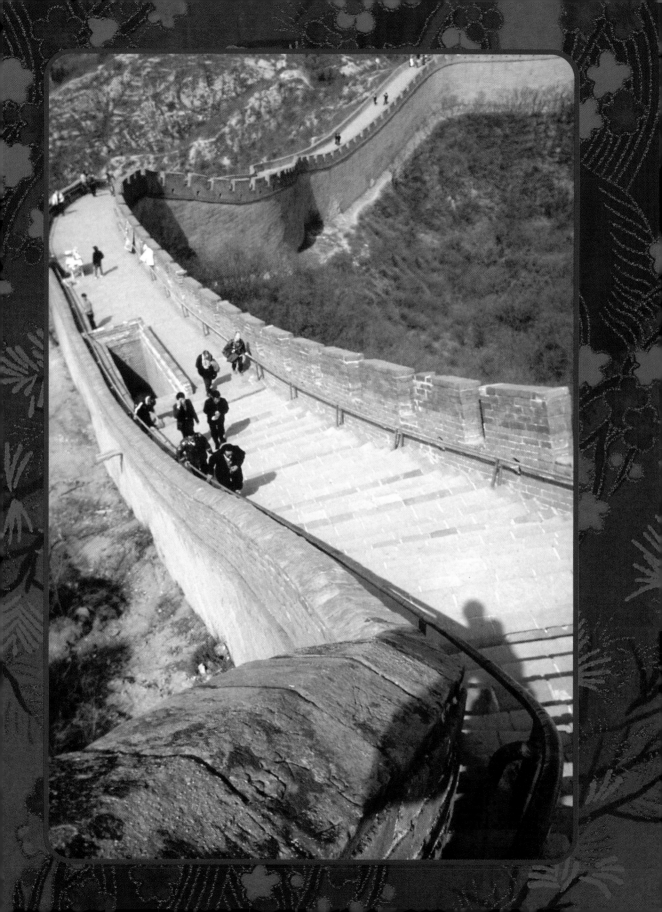

Visitors walk along a section of the Great Wall, an ancient wonder built by Qin Shihuang to protect his realm from barbarian attacks. In 221 B.C. Qin Shihuang established China's first unified empire.

3

# The First Emperor of China

"He who has not reached the Great Wall," a century-old Chinese saying goes, "is not a true man." The Great Wall, the result of one of the most remarkable construction projects in history (it remains the largest man-made structure ever built), stretches several thousand miles across northern China. Appropriately, the man who built China's most enduring symbol—Qin Shihuang (Ch'in Shih-huang)—also established the country's first unified empire, and the series of reforms he instituted produced profound and long-lasting influences on the Chinese culture.

## The Rise of Qin Shihuang

To understand the importance of Qin Shihuang, one must first know a bit about the times into which he was born. The future emperor, born Yingzheng (Ying-cheng), entered the world some 300 years after Confucius's birth. By this time, the Zhou dynasty—weak even during the great sage's lifetime—had further declined in power. The Zhou kings by the middle of the third century B.C. were merely religious leaders to whom the feudal lords paid tribute during worship ceremonies. Warfare between feudal states continued as before, but now only seven independent states remained, the smaller and weaker having gradually been taken over by the more powerful. This was near the end of the period in Chinese history known as the Warring States (475–221 B.C.).

Of the seven states struggling for supremacy, Qin (Ch'in) was the most powerful. Encompassing roughly the same territory as today's Shaanxi Province, Qin enjoyed a strategic location: its vast, fertile land was shielded by tall mountains with narrow, easily guarded passes. But geography was not the only reason for the rise of Qin power. Since the time of the Hundred Schools of Thought, the Qin rulers had adopted Legalism as the basis of state policy. Unlike Confucianism, which suggested that men should be governed primarily by the example of a virtuous ruler, Legalism held that men are by nature evil and must be governed through the firm and impartial enforcement of strict, even draconian laws. This form of governance, combined with a series of successful economic reforms, had solidified the Qin rulers' control and transformed the state into a formidable military power.

The circumstances of Yingzheng's rise to power were quite extraordinary. His father, Zichu (Tzu-ch'u), was a disfavored prince of Qin. When Zichu was young, he had been sent to the state of Zhao (Chao) as a hostage; this gesture was meant to demonstrate Qin's goodwill toward its neighbor. Sizing up the situation, a rich merchant in Zhao named Lü Buwei (Lü Pu-wei) recognized an opportunity. He first befriended Zichu. Then, by skillfully using his wealth, he contrived to free the hostage and succeeded in having the disfavored royal son return to Qin as the crown prince.

When Zichu became infatuated with his favorite concubine, Lü Buwei stepped aside and let the prince take her back to Qin as his wife. In 259 B.C., shortly after Zichu had returned to Qin, Yingzheng was born to the former concubine of Lü Buwei. Historians are not certain whether the merchant or the prince was Yingzheng's natural father, but one thing is clear: Lü Buwei had carved out a niche for himself in Qin for years to come.

In time, Zichu—with Lü Buwei serving as his councilor—succeeded to the throne of Qin and became King Zhuangxiang (Chuang-hsiang). His reign lasted only three years, however. Upon his death in 247 B.C., Yingzheng, who was 13 at the time, became the new king. Lü Buwei, appointed the grand councilor, governed

**This silk painting, from a 17th-century Chinese book, shows Emperor Qin Shihuang being carried on a palanquin, or covered throne. Qin Shihuang conducted several inspection tours of his empire during his 11-year reign.**

Qin for a decade until he was banished and replaced with another adviser, Li Si (Li Ssu).

Under the capable administration of Lü Buwei and Li Si, the state of Qin became increasingly strong, and Yingzheng also grew into a powerful king. The Qin troops, led by the able general Meng Tian (Meng T'ien), stormed across China. In 256 B.C. Qin forced the Zhou king to give up his throne, thus officially ending the Zhou dynasty. In the following decades, Qin eliminated the remaining independent states one after another. In 221 B.C. Qin conquered the state of Qi (Ch'i), thereby gaining control over the entire territory of what was then China.

After five centuries of constant warfare, China was for the first time united under one central power. Now Yingzheng ruled over an immense empire of more than 1 million square miles. To the Chinese of the time, this constituted the entire civilized world. Yingzheng felt that the title of "king" was no longer sufficient to describe the elevated position he had attained. Drawing on the titles of ancient kings and heroes, he invented a new title for himself: *shihuangdi* (*shih-huang-ti*), which literally means "First Sovereign Emperor." Proclaiming himself the First Emperor of Qin, Yingzheng—who would thereafter become known to history as Qin Shihuang—declared that his family would rule China for "10,000 generations."

## China's First Unified Empire

The new Qin empire stretched north and west to the Gobi Desert, south to present-day Vietnam, and east to the sea. Qin Shihuang faced the formidable task of governing this vast empire, which was bordered by no other civilized nations. A man of great vision, the First Emperor immediately began to institute a series of political, social, and economic reforms to consolidate his authority.

To ensure that his dynasty would avoid the fate of the Zhou kings, whose power fell into the hands of the feudal lords they set up to govern their territory, Qin Shihuang decided to completely abandon the hereditary feudal system. He divided his empire into new administrative areas of 36 *jun* (*chün*), or commanderies, which were subdivided into *xian* (*hsien*), or prefectures. Each commandery was governed by three officials: a civil administrator, a military governor, and an inspector. These officials were appointed by the imperial court in Qin's capital, Xianyang (Hsien-yang)—about 15 miles west of present-day Xi'an (Hsi-an)—and reported directly to the emperor. Locally, these officials shared authority in a system of checks and balances, and the emperor could remove them at any time and for any reason. This form of centralized bureaucratic government would become the basic administrative system of China until the early 20th century.

At the beginning of his rule, Qin Shihuang had to deal with the former feudal kingdoms' numerous royal families. He moved them all to his capital, where, detached from their land and people and under the emperor's close supervision, they posed little threat to his power. As further insurance against rebellion by the conquered states, Qin Shihuang had all their metal weapons taken to Xianyang. There, according to *Shi Ji* (*Shih Chi*), or *The Historical Records*, the weapons were melted down and recast as bells and bell supports, or made into 12 giant human statues. Each statue weighed thousands of pounds and was put in the imperial palace.

Qin Shihuang also ordered the construction of more than 4,000 miles of trunk roads, which radiated from his capital to various outposts of the empire. With this extensive network of roads, he could send his armies across the empire very quickly to put down any local rebellions.

Qin, once considered a "barbarous state," had risen to power upon the principles of Legalism, one of which was to standardize. In order to control and administer his huge empire, Qin Shihuang immediately established a standard code of strict laws. In addition, he unified various aspects of social and economic life. In the past, each of the seven feudal kingdoms of the Warring States period had had its own writing system, measures, and currency, which now created great confusion in the unified empire. Qin Shihuang banned all regional variations of the written language and adopted the *xiaozhuan* (*hsiao chuan*) and *lishu* (*li shu*) scripts formulated by Grand Councilor Li Si as the standard writing system. Weights, lengths, and volumes were also standardized to promote trade and commerce. The different coins in use in the former warring kingdoms were now banned, and the Qin coin, round-shaped with a square hole in the middle, became the standard currency. Even axle width was standardized so that wagons could travel smoothly on the empire's roads.

The best-known achievement of Qin Shihuang is of course the Great Wall. Although his armies were fierce, Qin Shihuang was unable to conquer the steppe peoples roaming to the north and west of his realm. To combine the territories of various former kingdoms, he had already had the walls between the former warring states destroyed. Now, in order to defend his empire from attack by the "barbarians" in the north and west, Qin Shihuang commissioned his general Meng Tian to build a defensive wall across the northern frontier. A force of laborers, prisoners, and soldiers—totaling some 300,000, according to *The Historical Records*—was conscripted for this huge construction project.

**This bronze coin dates from the Qin dynasty, when Qin Shihuang mandated that a standard currency be used throughout his vast empire. Such coins remained in use in China until the early 20th century.**

For 12 years this labor force toiled on Qin's northern frontier—often under brutal conditions—constructing new segments and repairing and connecting existing walls. The final product, which Chinese refer to poetically as the "10,000-*li* Long Wall" (a *li* is a Chinese measurement equal to about 1/3 mile), stretched from the empire's northeastern shore to the northwestern city of Lintao (Lin-t'ao). The

**Although Qin Shihuang was a brilliant administrator, he was also a ruthless tyrant. This silk painting commemorates the most notorious incident from his reign: the burning of books and persecution of Confucian scholars (here doomed scholars are seen being thrown into a ravine at the bottom right).**

Great Wall completed the landward encirclement of the Qin empire.

Qin Shihuang was now the supreme ruler of an empire that was effectively cut off from the rest of the world. While his physical control was virtually unchallengeable, he endeavored to extend his power even to the minds of his subjects. In 213 B.C., when some scholars lamented the end of hereditary feudalism and praised the wise, virtuous kings of the remote past, Qin Shihuang grew furious, interpreting the scholars' statements as implied criticism of his rule. On the advice of Li Si, his grand councilor, he ordered the burning of all books in the empire, particularly those dealing with competing philosophies such as Confucianism. The only exceptions were historical records of Qin, the Legalist writings, and books on agriculture and medicine. Fortunately, copies of the banned books were kept in the imperial library. The next year, he buried 460 Confucian scholars alive in Xianyang to forever silence them from "using the past to discredit the present." More scholars were banished to remote areas, including Crown Prince Fusu (Fu-su), who had protested against some of the emperor's harsh policies. To prevent a free spread of ideas, Qin Shihuang also banned private teaching, which had started in Confucius's time.

## Death of the First Emperor

Qin Shihuang believed that his dynasty would endure for countless generations and that his great achievements would be revered by people in "all four seas." However, the very harshness of his rule sowed the seeds of the Qin dynasty's doom. The lands he had conquered were full of people who resented his tyranny. Construction of the Great Wall and the empire's road system, as well a series of military campaigns undertaken to subdue the peoples at Qin's northern frontiers, had claimed tens of thousands of lives and caused untold human suffering. These ventures had also drained the treasury. Two attempts were made on the emperor's life; another assassination attempt had occurred before the unification of China. Although all failed to harm him physically, their psychological impact was obvious. Qin Shihuang put his empire under tighter control and sought various ways to achieve immortality. He drank mercury, which the ancient Chinese believed would make a person live longer, and he twice sent large expeditions out to the East Sea in search of the elixir of life. All these efforts were in vain. In 210 B.C. Qin Shihuang died on an inspection tour of his empire.

At that time, Crown Prince Fusu was still banished to the northern frontier, where he was supervising the construction of the Great Wall. Grand Councilor Li Si and Qin Shihuang's favorite eunuch, Zhao Gao (Chao Kao), who were accompanying the emperor on his tour, conspired to put the second of Qin Shihuang's sons, Huhai (Hu-hai), on the throne. They prevented news of the emperor's death from becoming known and had the body hidden in a chariot. Each day on the way back to the capital, food and daily reports were brought into the chariot as usual, as though the emperor were still alive. To disguise the odor of the dead body, they put a cart of salted fish behind the chariot. When they finally made it back to the capital, Li Si and Zhao Gao issued an imperial order for both Prince Fusu and his supporter General Meng Tian to commit suicide, and successfully installed Huhai as Ershi Huangdi (Erh Shih Huang Ti), the Second Emperor.

Weak of personality, Huhai had none of his father's ability and vision. The powerful empire Qin Shihuang built to last "10,000 generations" barely extended beyond his lifetime. Within three years, revolts broke out across the country, and the Second Emperor was soon killed. In 206 B.C. one of the rebellion leaders, Liu Bang (Liu Pang), started a new dynasty called Han, which would rule China for the next 400 years.

During the mid-1970s, farmers digging a well stumbled upon some terra-cotta figures near Xi'an. In the years that followed, Chinese archaeologists uncovered a huge army of terra-cotta soldiers, created more than 22 centuries ago to guard the tomb of China's first emperor.

## Qin Shihuang's Legacy

The quick rise and fall of the Qin empire was soon the subject of analysis and debate. Confucian scholars, who believed in ruling by virtue, prevailed over the Legalists during the Han dynasty. They looked upon Qin Shihuang as a tyrant who had set his own doom by harsh laws and total lack of care for his people. They attacked him for his suspicious origins and ridiculed him for his futile search for immortality.

The achievements of Qin Shihuang, however, should not be obscured by the Confucian criticism. Many of his reforms had enduring and far-reaching effects on China. It was he who created the first unified empire following hundreds of years of war, thereby establishing the concept of unification in the minds of all future generations. Although China would later split into parts at certain points of its history, a unified country has always been the goal of every ruler. It was also Qin Shihuang who established the model of centralized administration that was to be followed by all succeeding dynasties. The Great Wall, although built at the cost of tremendous human suffering, was an effective defense against foreign invasions for many dynasties and is today the most enduring symbol of China. Thanks to Qin Shihuang's standardization of the writing system, the cultural integrity of the country was preserved despite many later political breakdowns. While various regional dialects are spoken today throughout China, the written script remains the same for everyone, enabling people from all regions to communicate with one another.

Nearly 2,200 years after his death, Qin Shihuang attracted the attention not just of China, but of the whole world. In 1974 farmers digging a well about 20 miles east of Xi'an stumbled upon what turned out to be a gigantic army of terra-cotta soldiers guarding the First Emperor's nearby tomb. Since that time, archaeologists have uncovered more than 7,000 of these life-sized clay soldiers, each with unique physical characteristics. Historical records suggest that construction of this army, along with Qin Shihuang's complex tomb, which has yet to be excavated, began when he first ascended the throne in 247 B.C. and lasted beyond his death 37 years later. Today the terra-cotta army stands in mute witness to the power of the First Emperor and the immeasurable legacy he left to China.

The Big Wild Goose Pagoda, which dates to the mid-seventh century, is part of a Buddhist temple complex near Xi'an. It was rebuilt and enlarged during the reign of Empress Wu Zetian, who ruled China from A.D. 690 to 705.

# 4

# China's Only Female Emperor

Throughout human history, women have played a subservient role to men in most cultures. China is no exception. Confucius, the philosopher who shaped Chinese thinking for thousands of years, grouped women with "petty men" (the opposite of "gentlemen"). "Of all people," the sage observed, "women and petty men are the most difficult to deal with."

In Confucian China, women hardly had any standing at all independent of men. Before she married, a woman had to obey her father. After marrying, she had to obey her husband (even though she'd probably had no role in deciding whom that man would be, as arranged marriages were the rule). In the event a woman outlived her husband, that still did not mean she became her own master; a widow had to obey her sons. A Chinese woman was generally nameless: she bore a combination of her maiden family name and her husband's family name. And up until the mid-20th century, a Chinese man could take as many wives at the same time as he pleased, whereas a Chinese woman had to remain loyal to her husband even after his death.

But during the Tang (T'ang) dynasty (618–907), one of the most prosperous periods in Chinese history, a woman named Wu Zetian (Wu Tse-t'ien) challenged these conventions. Not only did she make herself the head of state in the "Middle Kingdom," she also effectively ruled the empire for more than half a century. Her rule marked the only time in China's 5,000-year history that a woman held the throne in her own right.

## "The Charming Lady"

Wu Zetian was born in 624, at the beginning of the Tang dynasty. Her father was a rich timber merchant who had fought for Li Yuan (Li Yüan), the first emperor of Tang, in overthrowing the previous Sui dynasty (581–618). For his loyalty and bravery, he was awarded a high post in the government and a wife from a Sui noble family. Because of his changing posts, the Wu family moved from place to place when Wu Zetian was young.

Under the Tang rulers, social life was less rigid and conventional, and women enjoyed a higher degree of freedom, than under other Chinese dynasties. Wu Zetian, though a girl, was taught to write, play music, and read the Chinese classics. Soon she was known for her intelligence, wit, and beauty.

At the age of 14, she was taken into the imperial palace to be a minor concubine of Emperor Taizong (T'ai-tsung). Taizong was taken by her beauty and named her Meiniang (Mei-niang), meaning "the Charming Lady."

Yet Wu Zetian was no ordinary beauty. As the emperor was soon to find out, she was a girl of determination and iron will. Taizong had a wild horse that nobody could tame. Wu Zetian informed the emperor that she could control the animal as long as she had three things: an iron whip, an iron mace, and a dagger. She told him that if the iron whip did not bring the horse to obedience, she would use the iron mace to beat its head, and if that did not work, she would use the dagger to cut its throat.

Taizong assigned Wu Zetian to work in the imperial study, where she was introduced to official documents and became acquainted with affairs of state. It was during her 12 years of official service to Taizong, arguably the greatest of all Chinese emperors, that Wu Zetian first developed the skills that enabled her to assume power a decade later. It was also during this time that she got to know Taizong's designated successor, Crown Prince Li Zhi (Li Chih). The future emperor, three years Wu Zetian's junior, became infatuated with her beauty and talent. The two began an affair without Taizong's knowledge.

**Beautiful, intelligent, and ambitious, Wu Zetian rose from minor concubine to empress. After the death of her husband, Emperor Gaozong, she became the first woman to rule imperial China in her own right.**

When Taizong died in 649, Wu Zetian—together with the other concubines who hadn't produced any children for the emperor—was sent to Ganye (Kan-yeh) Temple to live out her life as a nun. This was certainly preferable to the fate that befell concubines during most other Chinese dynasties: they were typically buried alive with the

These clay figures, made during the Tang dynasty (618–907), depict women playing musical instruments. Though women enjoyed greater freedom during the Tang era than under previous dynasties, the paths open to them were still very restricted—which makes Wu Zetian's achievements all the more remarkable.

dead emperor. Nonetheless, consignment to a life of obscurity proved unbearable for the ambitious Wu Zetian, who was just 26 years old. She soon made contact with her old lover, Li Zhi, who had by now become the new emperor Gaozong (Kao-tsung). Over the next three years, Gaozong frequently visited Wu at Ganye Temple. In 652 he took her back to his palace as a concubine, an act often condemned by later Confucian historians of China, for Wu Zetian had now served both father and son.

## From Concubine to Empress

Within a year of her return to the palace, Wu Zetian gave birth to a son and named him Li Hong (Li Hung). Soon she gained Gaozong's trust by virtue of her intelligence and personality. However, she craved more power and authority and started to compete with Gaozong's empress, Wang, and his other favorite concubine, Xiaoshu (Hsiao-shu). Before long the weak-willed Gaozong had come under Wu Zetian's domination. In 654 Wu gave birth to a baby girl. She apparently strangled the infant herself but framed Empress Wang for the murder. Before long, Gaozong, taken in by Wu Zetian's story, ousted both Empress Wang and Xiaoshu, despite strong opposition from his court.

In 655 Gaozong consulted his court on promoting Wu Zetian to be his empress. He met with fierce opposition. The aristocrats, led by his uncle Zhangsun Wuji (Chang-sun Wu-chi), cited Wu's lowly origin (despite her father's high post, she was not from one of the great aristocratic clans) and the fact that she had been Taizong's concubine. But Gaozong proceeded with his plan nonetheless. Once installed as empress, Wu Zetian immediately put Empress Wang and Xiaoshu to death and exiled their families and supporters, thus permanently eliminating her rivals.

The next year, Wu Zetian's son Li Hong became Gaozong's crown prince. As the mother of the future emperor, Wu's power continued to grow. Recognizing that the old aristocratic clans were still against her, she made great efforts to gain supporters from outside these clans. Meanwhile, she gradually disposed of her political rivals, who were removed from office, exiled, or executed one after another. In 659 Wu Zetian finally had her revenge on Zhangsun Wuji, her major opponent at court: first she banished him and his family, and then she forced him to commit suicide.

In 660 Emperor Gaozong suffered a severe stroke that left him blind. In the aftermath, he relinquished control of all administrative matters to Wu Zetian, making her the virtual ruler of the Tang empire for the next 23 years.

In order to closely monitor her subjects, Wu Zetian set up a secret police and an informer system. She appointed cruel officials to eliminate any opposition to her authority. These officials employed all kinds of tortures to deal with those accused of plotting against Wu. Many high ministers and aristocrats, as well as commoners, were subject to their brutality.

Ruthless as she was, Wu Zetian proved a very competent ruler. Her great ability as an administrator, her courage, and her decisive character gradually won her the respect of the court. She moved Tang's capital east to Luoyang (Lo-yang) and named it the "Eastern Capital"—signifying a break with the old aristocratic rule in Tang's "Western Capital," Xi'an, and a shift toward administration by scholar-officials. In 668 Tang forces conquered Korea and set up a provincial capital in Pyongyang. In 674 Wu Zetian announced what was called the "Twelve Suggestions," the first of a series of policies aimed at winning the support of the common people and of officials of lower status. These dozen suggestions, which included the encouragement of agriculture and silk production, tax reduction, and a disbandment of armies, reformed various aspects of economic, military, social, and political life.

In 674 Gaozong declared himself the "Heavenly Emperor" and Wu Zetian the "Heavenly Empress." Yet Wu Zetian's ambition extended beyond such a title, which was designed to distinguish her from all past empresses. She continued to remove potential rivals, including her own relatives. In 675 Crown Prince Li Hong died suddenly while accompanying his parents on a trip. It is generally believed that Wu Zetian poisoned her son because of his support for some of her enemies. Wu replaced him with her second son, Li Xian (Li Hsien).

## The "Holy and Divine Emperor"

Emperor Gaozong finally died in 683, after ruling mostly in name for 30 years. According to his final instructions, all important matters of state were to be decided by the Heavenly Empress. However, Crown Prince Li Xian ascended the throne as Zhongzong (Chung-tsung). Within two years Wu Zetian had deposed him and placed her fourth son, Ruizong (Jui-tsung), on the throne. Ruizong was merely a puppet emperor; actual power rested completely in the hands of Wu Zetian.

Soon Tang loyalists fomented a revolt, but it took Wu Zetian barely three months to quell the uprising. Another revolt by the Tang princes broke out a few years later, after Wu Zetian had declared herself the "Holy Mother Divine Empress," but it was crushed even faster. Wu used this second revolt as an opportunity to exile and execute many of Tang's imperial family members, and her authority as the supreme ruler of the empire was further strengthened.

By the year 690, all of Wu Zetian's political rivals had been removed, exiled, or put to death, and her rule had been solidified through years of effective administration. The 65-year-old empress was now ready to ascend the

Indian visitors stand in front of an enormous statue of the Vairocana Buddha at the Longmen Grotto near Luoyang. Wu Zetian is said to have been the model for this statue's face. As emperor she made Buddhism the state religion and ordered the construction of many Buddhist temples.

throne herself. She declared the start of a new empire of her own called Zhou (Chou), set her capital in Luoyang, and conferred upon herself the title "Holy and Divine Emperor." She would reign for the next 15 years, the only female emperor in Chinese history to rule in her own right.

Judging that her position was secure, the "Holy and Divine Emperor" turned against the cruel officials she had earlier appointed. One by one they were put to death, and the focus of the administration shifted to economic and cultural development.

Determined to break the dominance of the military and political aristocracy, Wu Zetian enlisted talented people from lower ranks who would in turn remain loyal to her. She revised the imperial civil service examinations and personally interviewed candidates for various government posts, which became the practice of emperors in all coming dynasties. Many of her excellent ministers, such as Yao Chong (Yao Ch'ung) and Song Jing (Sung Ching), were recruited in this way. They remained in court after her death and through their capable administration ensured continuing greatness for the Tang dynasty. Wu Zetian also encouraged talented people to volunteer their services. As some historians have noted, while her motives were to secure her own authority, these policies had great historical significance: they promoted the transformation of Chinese society from one dominated by the aristocracy to one governed by a class of scholar-administrators.

Wu Zetian also attached great importance to the development of agriculture. She ordered the construction of irrigation systems, encouraged people to cultivate new farmland, had textbooks on agriculture compiled, and reduced taxes.

Under the reign of Wu Zetian, Chinese Buddhism achieved its highest development. She established Buddhism as the state religion and had numerous Buddhist temples built. Many of the finest Buddhist cave sculptures were created during this time. The most famous are at Longmen (Lung-men), near Luoyang, where a colossal statue of the Vairocana Buddha stands more than 55 feet high. Its face is said to have been modeled after that of Wu Zetian.

As she grew older, Wu Zetian felt the pressure to select an heir. In 698 she restored her second son, Li Xian—whom she had sent into exile 14 years earlier—as crown prince, but she continued to rule the empire. In 705 she was forced by her court to relinquish the throne to Li Xian, who resumed his reign as Zhongzong and changed the name of the dynasty back to Tang.

**These stone attendants stand watch before the burial mound of Empress Wu and her husband, Emperor Gaozong.**

Wu Zetian was now 82 years old, and her health quickly deteriorated. She died at the end of the year.

## A Blank Tombstone

Wu Zetian was buried with her husband, Gaozong, in the Qianling (Ch'ien-ling) Tomb, located west of Xi'an. Following her wishes, her tombstone was left blank. Some interpreted this as a symbol of her absolute power, which went beyond words; others believed that Wu wanted future generations to decide for themselves how she should be evaluated.

Confucius had said that having a woman rule would be as unnatural as "having a hen crow like a rooster at daybreak." Wu Zetian proved to the Chinese that, in the intricate and difficult world of statecraft, a woman could be every bit as effective as a man—if given the opportunity.

Chinese civilization has always had a refined aesthetic sensibility, but the Song period produced some especially notable artistic achievements, including exquisite porcelain objects such as the green-and-black vase shown here. Poetry also reached a high point in the Song dynasty, and no poet from that time is more beloved and revered than Su Dongpo.

# 5

# A Beloved Poet

Actions, the old maxim says, speak louder than words. Over the broad sweep of human history, however, this is not always the case. For while the deeds of long-ago kings and queens, emperors, generals, and explorers are frequently forgotten, the words of great writers endure. They reach across the centuries, offering truth and beauty, ideas and insights, to countless generations. Great literature is indeed timeless.

Chinese literature begins with *Shi Jing* (*Shih Ching*), the *Book of Poems*; Confucius is said to have studied and memorized this collection of ancient verses.

As the Chinese nation developed, its literature, not surprisingly, also changed and evolved. Different periods in Chinese history are known for their distinct literary styles and characteristic literary personalities. But it is generally agreed that the most vibrant time for

Chinese literature was during the Tang (618–907) and Song (960–1279) dynasties, when poetry was the leading literary form. Household names such as Li Bai and Du Fu (Tu Fu) lived in the Tang period, the golden age of Chinese culture. And in the Song dynasty, three members of the same family, a father and two sons, made their names in both literature and politics. They were called "the Three Sus," in reference to their family name. This chapter is about the elder son, Su Dongpo (Su Tung-p'o), the greatest writer of the Song dynasty and one of the most beloved Chinese poets of all time.

## Life and Times of the Poet

Su Dongpo was born Su Shi (Su Shih) in Meishan (Mei-shan), located in present-day Sichuan (Ssu-ch'uan) Province, in the year 1036. This was early in the Song dynasty, one of the most prosperous and peaceful times in Chinese history. Culturally, the art of painting reached its zenith, and Song porcelain pieces were renowned for their elegant and exquisite beauty. The invention of movable type for printing greatly promoted all branches of scholarship and literature.

Su Shi's father, Su Xun (Su Hsün), was a late bloomer who didn't begin serious literary studies until he was 27. Unsuccessful at the imperial civil service exams, he fixed his hopes on his sons, Su Shi and Su Zhe (Su Che), beginning their education very early. The elder of the brothers by three years, Su Shi was sent at age eight to a private school run by a Taoist priest, where he soon became a favorite student. For a few years, while his father was away traveling, Su Shi's mother took up his education at home. Herself a well-educated woman from a prominent family, she undoubtedly had a great influence upon her son's development. When Su Shi was nine, she read to him the biography of Fan Pang (Fan P'ang), a fearless and righteous patriot in the Later Han dynasty (25–220) who repeatedly offended the court with his harsh, truthful words and was put to

Nature has traditionally served as a wellspring of inspiration for Chinese philosophers, scholars, and poets, including Su Dongpo. This waterside pavilion at Suzhou, built during Su Dongpo's time, served as a retreat where artists and thinkers could contemplate the beauty and grandeur of the natural world.

death as a result. Upon finishing the story, little Su Shi turned to his mother and asked her if he could one day become another Fan Pang. This episode, recorded in many of Su's biographies, demonstrates his determined, courageous character even at a young age.

In 1056 Su Shi and Su Zhe—now 20 and 17, respectively—traveled to Kaifeng (K'ai-feng) accompanied by their father. The brothers' purpose in journeying to the Song capital was to take the imperial civil service examinations. These were the same exams their father had earlier failed. Both brothers, however, passed with distinction. The following year, both passed a second exam, administered by the emperor himself at the imperial palace, and received the title *jinshi*

Su Dongpo married his first wife in 1054, when she was 15 years old. She died 11 years later, and he wrote the following poem in 1075, 10 years after her death.

# A Riverside Town*

Dreaming of my deceased wife on the night of the 20th day of the 1st moon

For ten long years the living of the dead knows nought.

> Should the dead be forgot
>
> And to mind never brought?

Her lonely grave is a thousand miles away.

To whom can I my grief convey?

Revived e'en if she be, could she still know me?

> My face is worn with care
>
> And frosted is my hair.

Last night I dreamed of coming to my native place:

> She's making up her face
>
> At the window with grace.

We gazed at each other hushed,

But tears from our eyes gushed.

When I am woken, I fancy her heart-broken

> Each night when the moon shines
>
> On the mound clad with pines.

*All poems in this chapter are from *Su Dong Po—a New Translation*. Translated by Xu Yuan Zhong. Hong Kong: The Commercial Press, 1982.

(*chin shih*), an honor bestowed only on those few scholars who passed the most rigorous level of the civil service examinations. Meanwhile, their father had presented some essays he had written to prominent scholar-officials in the capital and had gained wide recognition for his literary ability. Thus, within a year of their arrival in the capital, Su Xun and his sons had made their names and became known as the Three Sus.

Just when the Three Sus were about to start their political careers, in 1057, Su Shi's mother died. The father and sons immediately journeyed back home, where they observed the customary 27-month-long mourning that was required by Confucian traditions. In 1060 the three traveled to the capital again, where Su Xun received an official appointment and Su Shi and Su Zhe were appointed to posts in the provinces. The Three Sus thus began careers that were to make them famous in Chinese literary and political history.

From 1061 to 1065, Su Shi served as assistant magistrate in Fengxiang (Feng-hsiang), a poor frontier county bordering Song's threatening neighbor Xixia (Hsi-hsia). In 1065, after his term was over, Su Shi returned to the capital. Soon thereafter, his wife of 11 years died. The following year, as Su Shi waited in the capital for a new appointment, his father also died. He and his brother accompanied Su Xun's body home and buried their father with their mother, after which they again observed the 27-month mourning period in Meishan. This would be their last trip home, as their official posts and later their banishment forced them to travel constantly from place to place.

In 1069 Su Shi and Su Zhe went back to the capital, where they occupied posts for a brief time. A new emperor had just succeeded to the throne and had appointed a new prime minister named Wang Anshi (Wang An-shih). Wang, an accomplished poet and essayist himself, was a radical statesman. As soon as he came into

This watercolor painting on silk shows a Song dynasty emperor and various officials. Although obtaining a civil service position represented the highest aspiration available to most Chinese men in imperial China, factional squabbles and palace intrigues were an ever-present danger. In 1079 Su Dongpo fell victim to such political maneuvering. Charged with slandering the emperor, he was arrested, imprisoned, and later sent into exile.

power, he initiated a series of dramatic reforms known as the "New Laws." Having worked in the provinces, Su Shi understood the hardships these new policies would cause for the peasants. He joined conservative officials in openly criticizing the New Laws and soon fell out of favor with the emperor and with Wang Anshi's influential faction at court. As a result, he was sent to a subordinate post at Hangzhou (Hang-chou), where he stayed for three years, and then assigned to a series of lesser provincial posts.

In 1079 Su Shi was charged with slandering the emperor and was arrested at the capital. After a 130-day imprisonment, he was banished to Huangzhou (Huang-chou) in today's Hubei (Hu-pei) Province, where he lived in harsh conditions and had to farm for a living. He cultivated a piece of land on the eastern slope of the city and called himself Dongpo Jushi (Tung-p'o Chu Shih), "the Master of the Eastern Slope." From then on, Dongpo became his preferred literary name, and people called him Su Dongpo. Despite all the hardships, it was in Huangzhou that Su Dongpo wrote many of his masterpieces.

When the emperor died in 1085, the conservative force at court came to power with a young emperor and overthrew the New Laws party. This incident directly affected Su Dongpo's political career, as he was immediately transferred to a high provincial post and soon after recalled to the capital, where he was promoted three times in a year. In 1086, at age 49, he was appointed *hanlin*, a high official at court, and took charge of drafting imperial orders. For a short period, Su Dongpo enjoyed peace.

However, he soon fell out of favor with the conservatives who now dominated the court. Deeply concerned about the plight of the common people, Su Dongpo had never been afraid to voice his opinions about how government policies affected ordinary Chinese—even when doing so was not politically advisable. While he had earlier opposed the New Laws, he came to believe that some of these policies actually worked well and should be kept. This stance did not endear him to the conservatives.

But with yet another new emperor in 1093, the political climate shifted once more. The New Laws party regained power, and in 1094 Su Dongpo—now 58 and in poor health—found himself banished for a second time, to the remote Huizhou (Hui-chou) in Guangdong (Kuang-tung). His second wife had died the previous year, but Su Dongpo was accompanied on this last and hardest journey of his life by his youngest son, Su Guo (Su Kuo)—who later became an accomplished poet in his own right—and by his concubine Wang Zhaoyun (Wang Chao-yün). For many years she had been Su Dongpo's muse.

In 1097 Su Dongpo was ordered farther south, to the island of Hainan, which was then an undeveloped land populated by aborigines. In 1100 he was finally permitted to return to the mainland and restored to office. He decided to live out the rest of his days in Changzhou (Ch'ang-chou), located in Zhejiang (Che-chiang) Province, and pleaded with the court to allow him to retire. However, not long after he arrived in Changzhou, he fell seriously ill. He passed away in June of 1101 at the age of 66.

# Reasons for Su Dongpo's Fame

In many ways Su Dongpo represented the ideal of a Confucian scholar-official in imperial China. His chosen career brought him into close contact with common people as he went from place to place for his various government posts, and he never failed to display Confucian benevolence, or *ren*. He had a deep sympathy for his fellow human beings, and he worked hard to improve people's lives. In Hangzhou he drilled many wells so that people would have clean water to drink. He organized successful flood and famine relief in various places, mined coal in Xuzhou (Hsü-chou), and taught the aborigines in Hainan to clear away the jungle and cultivate farmland. His deep concern for the well-being of the common people was reflected in such poems as "Lament of a Peasant Woman" and "Snow on New Year's Day." He was a great humanitarian and a friend of the people.

Su Dongpo was also a man of integrity and courage. Although his extreme outspokenness frequently got him into trouble, he never compromised his principles for political gain. For that he was exiled

In China calligraphy is a much-admired art form, and the Chinese particularly esteem poets accomplished at rendering their works in beautiful, balanced calligraphic characters. Su Dongpo was a master calligrapher, and his original works are considered artful both for the fluency of their verse and for the beauty of the brushed characters.

twice, the second time at an advanced age. Su Dongpo could be angered, but he never seems to have hated or held grudges against people. This is perhaps best illustrated by his relationship with Wang Anshi, who had him banished for five years. Despite their political disagreements, Su Dongpo remained friendly with the leader of the New Laws party, and in his later years he went out of his way to visit Wang Anshi and exchange many poems with him.

There is an incurable optimism in Su Dongpo that people continue to regard with fondness. He had plenty of reasons to be bitter: because of his principles he suffered imprisonment, banishment, and physical hardship; he also endured separation from his homeland and his beloved brother, Su Zhe. Yet he never gave in to bitterness or pessimism. Every now and then his Taoist sense of detachment would emerge in poems such as the following:

> I long regret I am not master of my own.
>
> When can I ignore the hums of up and down?
>
> In the still night the soft winds quiver
>
> On the ripples of the river.
>
> From now on, I would vanish with my little boat,
>
> For the rest of my life, on the sea I would float.

But in Su Dongpo this Taoist detachment from life is blended, in a wonderful combination, with the Confucian commitment to life. His interests were remarkably broad. A distinguished painter, he pioneered a new style called "scholar painting." He was also a master calligrapher, and from his lifetime onward collectors have pursued his every piece, including random notes. Su Dongpo was an engineer who conducted projects on lakes and mines, an experimenter in wine making, and a gourmet cook who composed many poems on how to prepare certain dishes (today a famous dish in the Sichuan style of cooking still bears his name).

In spite of all these accomplishments, however, it should be noted that Su Dongpo is known principally as a poet and writer, and his works have brought pleasure to people for a thousand years. He experimented with almost every form in traditional Chinese literature—poetry, prose, state essays, commentaries on the Confucian classics—and he excelled in all. Yet he is best remembered for his poetry, both the *shi* (*shih*) and *ci* (*tz'u*) forms, and his prose poetry (*fu*). While the *shi* is as old as Chinese literature itself—beginning with the *Book of Poems*—the *ci* was a new style, developed only in the late Tang dynasty. The *ci* were originally lyrics written to accompany well-known tunes. Before Su Dongpo's time, they dealt mostly with overly sentimental themes and were considered less respectable than the *shi*. It was Su Dongpo who first employed the *ci* to treat many of the same themes he did in his *shi*. Because he was such a good writer, he elevated the *ci* to a status as high as that of the *shi* and ushered in its golden age in the Song dynasty.

To read Su Dongpo's poems in the original Chinese is a sublime delight, but as his biographer Lin Yutang (Lin Yu-t'ang) well noted, Su Dongpo's writings have a quality that is difficult to explain, much less feel in translation. Nonetheless, a translation of his most famous *ci*, "Memories of the Past at Red Cliff," may give readers a glimpse of his genius, which eclipsed all before and after him:

> The Great River eastward flows,
>
> With its waves are gone all those
>
> Gallant heroes of bygone years.
>
> West of the ancient fortress appears
>
> The Red Cliff where General Zhou won his early fame
>
> When the Three Kingdoms were in flame.
>
> Jagged rocks tower in the air,

Swashing waves beat on the shore,

Rolling up a thousand heaps of snow.

To match the hills and the river so fair,

How many heroes of yore

Made a great show!


I recall those years when Zhou Yu was at the height

Of his success, so brave and so bright,

Newly wedded to a young lady fair.

In a silk hood, with a plume fan in hand,

He laughed and jested and

Enemy ships were destroyed like castles in the air.

If his soul should come back today,

He would be moved to laugh and say

Before my time my hair's turned gray.

Life is but like a dream,

I would fain drink to the moon on the stream.


Su Dongpo's literary accomplishments alone would be enough to guarantee him a seat among the greatest Chinese who ever lived. Yet he has also won the admiration of every succeeding generation of Chinese for his remarkable character—his love of life, his compassion for the common people, his courageous stands for his principles. In 1170, long after his death, the Song emperor Xiaozong (Hsiao-tsung) honored him with the title *Wenzhong Gong*, "Literary Patriotic Duke," and expressed the following in his imperial announcement: "We regret not being born at the same time with him in order to make full use of his talents." People today feel very much the same way.

This woodcut from an old Chinese manuscript shows one of the ships of Zheng He, the admiral whose epic voyages opened up the Indian Ocean to trade with China during the first half of the 15th century.

# Admiral of the "Treasure Fleets"

The last quarter of the 15th century was a period of great maritime exploration. Lucrative trade opportunities in the Far East beckoned the European powers. Goods such as silks and spices were in great demand in Europe, but the overland route to China, the Silk Road, was fraught with difficulty and danger. Portugal and Spain sought a sea route to the Far East that would replace the Silk Road. In that quest, the Portuguese navigator Bartolomeu Dias sailed south along the western coast of Africa and rounded the Cape of Good Hope in 1488; 10 years later his countryman Vasco da Gama would complete the route by sailing across the Indian Ocean and reaching India's Calicut. In 1492, sailing under the Spanish flag and seeking a westward route to the Orient, Christopher Columbus landed in the Americas. This, of course, opened European exploration and colonization

of the New World, though Columbus himself went to his grave convinced that he had reached the islands off the Asian coast. It wasn't until 30 years later that Ferdinand Magellan would fulfill Columbus's dream of reaching the China seas by sailing west. Today Magellan, Columbus, and other European explorers are household names.

Little does the world remember that 70 years before Vasco da Gama made it to East Africa on his way to India, a Chinese admiral commanding a fleet 90 times bigger had reached the same spot from the other side of the world. In fact, between 1405 and 1433, this admiral, a eunuch named Zheng He (Cheng Ho), led a total of seven maritime expeditions into the Indian Ocean in the service of China's Ming dynasty (1368–1644). He reached more than 30 countries in areas as distant as the Persian Gulf, the Red Sea, and the east coast of Africa. His "Treasure Fleets," as they were called, dwarfed any flotilla that had come before or would come after for a long time: Zheng He's expeditions brought together 48 to more than 200 ships, and in total his smallest expedition carried some 25,000 crew members and specialists.

**When Christopher Columbus sighted land on his 1492 voyage, he believed he had sailed to China. Not until later did Europeans realize that Columbus had actually stumbled upon a continent whose existence they had previously been unaware of.**

## Early Life

The year 1368 marked the end of the Yuan (Yüan) dynasty in China; the Mongol empire had been established about a century earlier by the powerful troops of Genghis Khan. In its place was a new dynasty called Ming, whose first emperor, Zhu Yuanzhang (Chu Yüan-chang), rose from the ranks of the commoners.

It was at this transitional time in Chinese history that Zheng He was born into a Muslim family in the southwestern Chinese province of Yunnan (Yün-nan). Zheng He's original name was Ma He. The family name "Ma" is a Chinese version of Muhammad, the founder of the Islamic religion. Ma He's grandfather and his father had both made the hajj—the pilgrimage to Mecca, Islam's holiest city. From a very young age, Ma He had been fascinated by the accounts of their pilgrimage, and their stories of journeying through foreign lands would greatly inspire his own grand voyages many years later.

During Ma He's childhood, Yunnan was one of the last strongholds of the remaining Yuan forces. In 1381, when Ma He was 11 years old, the Ming emperor sent a large army there and reclaimed the area from the Yuan forces. During this conquest, Ma He was taken captive by the Ming armies. As was then customary with young male captives, he was castrated and sent to the imperial palace as a servant. Later he was given as a personal servant to Zhu Di (Chu Ti), the Ming prince of Yan (Yen). Unlike most other eunuchs, Ma He was able to obtain an education and learned the Confucian classics. He also learned the art of war while accompanying his master on military expeditions to eliminate the Mongol forces.

Zhu Di was the most able and ambitious of Emperor Zhu Yuanzhang's 26 sons. He commanded a large army and was stationed in today's Beijing area to defend against the Mongols in the north. In 1400 he revolted against his nephew, the emperor Jianwen (Chien-wen), who had succeeded to the throne after Zhu Yuanzhang's death. Zhu Di successfully deposed his nephew following a two-year civil war; he took the throne in 1402. During the civil war, Ma He had distinguished himself as a capable military commander, earning Zhu Di's confidence. As a reward, Zhu Di conferred on him the surname "Zheng"—a great honor in feudal China—and Ma He was thereafter known as Zheng He. Zheng He later converted to Buddhism and was also called Sanbao Taijian (San Pao T'ai Chien), "the Eunuch of Three Gems."

Family records show that Zheng He was tall and heavy with clear-cut features. He had long earlobes (which in the Chinese culture is a sign of extraordinary qualities), a stride like a tiger's, and a clear and vibrant voice.

## To Sail the "Western Oceans"

Under Zhu Di, who reigned from 1402 to 1424 as Emperor Yongle (Yung-lo), the "Eternal Happiness," China's war-devastated economy was soon restored. After settling down in his throne, Emperor Yongle was eager to display the might of his empire, so he commissioned the building of a large fleet. The fleet would sail to Xiyang (Hsi-yang), the "Western Oceans," which at that time referred to the vast area west of Borneo. The emperor appointed his favorite eunuch, Zheng He, as the commander-in-chief of the fleet, partly because of his extraordinary abilities and partly because of his Islamic and Buddhist beliefs, which were popular in the countries the fleet would visit.

China had a long history of maritime activities. As early as the third century B.C., the First Emperor of Qin had sent ships out to the East Sea to search for the elixir of immortality. Although nothing magical was found, the ships are believed to have reached Japan. By the time of the Yuan dynasty, China had established trade relationships with many countries in Southeast Asia.

By the end of the Yuan dynasty, the Chinese were able to build ships big enough to carry more than 1,000 people. Long-distance navigation was also facilitated by the use of a simple device that the Chinese had invented many centuries earlier: the compass. Historical records show that the magnetic compass—which the Chinese called *zhi nan zhen* (*chih nan chen*), the "south pointing needle"—was in use by the late third century B.C. By the late Song dynasty (960–1279), the Chinese had used this instrument widely in ocean navigation.

These technological developments had paved the way for Zheng He's grand voyages. But why did Emperor Yongle order such large-scale expeditions? It is generally believed that political considerations played a part in the emperor's decisions: the deposed Emperor Jianwen was said to be hiding somewhere in Southeast Asia with forces that remained loyal to him. Thus he might still pose a threat to Yongle's rule, and the emperor wanted to discover his whereabouts. Economically, Yongle wanted to extend China's trade relations farther than Southeast Asia and collect tribute from the "barbarian countries beyond the seas." As the ruler of the most powerful nation in the world, Yongle wanted to attract "all under heaven" to be civilized in Confucian harmony.

## Seven Epic Voyages

In 1405 the first expedition led by Zheng He set out from the Liujia (Liu-chia) port in Suzhou (Su-chou), on the east coast of China. The fleet consisted of 62 ships, 4 of which were called *baochuan* (*pao ch'uan*), or "treasure ships." These treasure ships, each about 400 feet long and 160 feet wide, were the largest vessels ever built to that point in history; they were almost four times longer than Columbus's flagship, the *Santa María*, which would sail the Atlantic Ocean more than 85 years later. The fleet also included horse ships carrying nothing but horses, water ships that carried fresh water for the crew, supply ships, and warships.

Under Zheng He's command in the great fleet were some 27,800 people. These included seven eunuchs, who served as the imperial representatives and ambassadors; sailors and navigators; secretaries who were to prepare official documents; military commanders and troops; astrologers, who were responsible for weather, calendar, and astronomical observations; translators and interpreters; cooks; Buddhist and Islamic priests; and almost 200 doctors, who were charged not only with taking care of the crew's health but also with collecting herbal medicines from overseas.

The first major city the Treasure Fleet sailed to was Chamba, in today's Vietnam. There the Chinese traded for ebony, lakawood, and aloe wood. When they sailed to Java, Zheng He was surprised to find large communities of rich Chinese merchants, who had arrived there at the end of the 14th century.

After trading silks and porcelains for spices and copper coins, the fleet sailed on to Ceylon (today's Sri Lanka). Upon finding that the king of Ceylon was not particularly friendly, they passed it by quickly.

Traveling around the southern tip of India, the fleet reached Calicut, at the time the biggest free port and a major trading center in the Indian Ocean. From late 1406 to the spring of 1407, the Treasure Fleet stayed in this "great country of the Western Oceans" and bartered and traded with the Indians for precious stones, pearls, coral, and peppers. The Chinese established such a good reputation in Calicut that in their later expeditions into the "Western Oceans," they always received a warm welcome there and were able to use it as a base for further voyages.

When the monsoons shifted direction in the spring of 1407, Zheng He's fleet sailed toward home. Envoys from Calicut, Malacca, and many Sumatra states boarded the Treasure Fleet on their tribute journey to the "Middle Kingdom." At the Strait of Malacca, the fleet was attacked by more than 5,000 pirates led by a Chinese chieftain named Chen Zuyi (Ch'en Tsu-i), who had fled from southern China some years earlier. Zheng He's troops

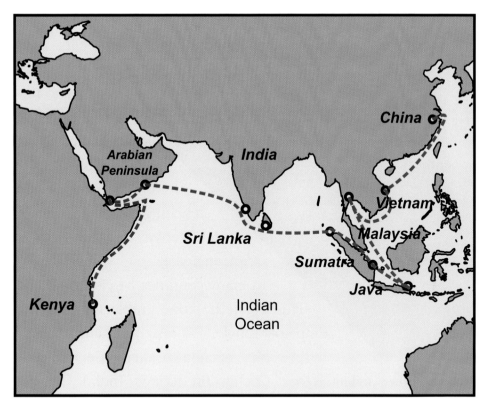

**The dotted line on this map shows the main route Zheng He followed in his expeditions to the "Western Oceans."**

defeated the pirates and captured Chen and some of his followers, whom they took back to the Ming capital Nanjing (Nanking), where they were executed.

Although Zheng He hadn't discovered the whereabouts of the deposed emperor Jianwen, Emperor Yongle was greatly pleased by the diplomatic and trade relations the eunuch admiral had established with various countries and the exotic goods he had brought back to China. From 1407 until his death in 1424, Yongle sent out five more voyages into the "Western Oceans," ordering Zheng He to go as far as he could to expand China's trade and diplomacy.

These five expeditions were organized on the same grand scale as the first one, with 48 to 249 ships and crews of 27,000 to 30,000. To provide a base for his long voyages, Zheng He built warehouses in

Malacca to store provisions, goods, tribute, and gifts from foreign lands. From there, his fleet ventured farther and farther into the Indian Ocean, exploring the Persian Gulf and the Red Sea, and finally reaching today's Somalia and Kenya on the eastern African coast.

In many countries he visited, Zheng He erected stone tablets glorifying Emperor Yongle. He also proclaimed countries such as Calicut, Ceylon, and Cochin (in today's India) Chinese subsidiaries. On each voyage, Zheng He carried a costly cargo of the famous blue-and-white Ming porcelains, silks, lacquerware, and fine-art objects. These he traded with foreign nations for treasures coveted in

**Zheng He and other sailors were able to navigate the seas with the help of the compass. First developed in China before the second century B.C., the compass was unknown to European navigators for another 1,200 years. Shown here is a combination compass and sundial that dates from the Ming dynasty.**

China: spices, precious stones, ivory, rhinoceros horn, tortoise shell, rare woods, incense, pearls, and carpets. He also brought back to the emperor exotic animals and birds considered auspicious by the Chinese, such as elephants, peacocks, leopards, and zebras. In 1415 the king of Malindi (in today's Kenya) went with Zheng He to Nanjing and presented Emperor Yongle with a giraffe. The Chinese believed the giraffe to be the legendary *qilin* (*ch'i lin*), the Chinese unicorn. The *qilin* was one of four sacred animals in China, along with the dragon, the phoenix, and the tortoise. According to legend, a *qilin* had appeared before Confucius's birth and spit out a tablet announcing that he would be the uncrowned king. Surely the appearance of a *qilin* at the Ming court now was a sign of a well-governed land under a virtuous ruler. Yongle and his imperial court were immensely pleased.

In addition to its successes in trade and diplomacy, the Treasure Fleet demonstrated and extended China's power. On his third voyage, after Ceylon attacked the fleet, Zheng He captured its king and queen and brought them back to Nanjing. Although Yongle reprimanded the monarchs, he spared their lives. On its fourth voyage, the Treasure Fleet helped put down a rebellion against the king in the city-state of Semudera in Sumatra.

Ever since Zheng He's first voyage, a steady flow of foreign envoys from the "Western Oceans" came to the Ming capital, bringing with them tribute to the emperor. China's influence was widely spread across Southeast Asia and the Indian Ocean.

By the time of Zheng He's seventh and final voyage, Emperor Yongle had already passed away. Yongle's grandson, the new emperor, wanted Zheng He to restore peaceful relations between Siam (today's Thailand) and the Malay kingdom of Malacca and to resume trade relations with countries in the "Western Oceans." On this expedition Zheng He is believed to have reached Mecca and fulfilled his duty as a Muslim. He died on the return voyage in 1433.

## The End of an Era

After Zheng He's death, China stopped its grand ocean explorations. The scholar-officials at the Ming court criticized the great cost of Zheng He's voyages—which, according to them, had accomplished nothing except to bring back to China exotic but generally useless items. These scholar-officials convinced the new emperor to turn to domestic affairs instead. Eventually, the Ming rulers would order the destruction of China's largest oceangoing ships and pursue a policy of self-imposed isolation. This proved a fateful decision. Within 50

**On his final voyage Zheng He is believed to have reached Mecca, the city on the Arabian Peninsula that contains Islam's most sacred shrine (the Kaaba, the square black building pictured in the center of this photograph).**

years, European explorers would begin sailing to all parts of the world, and in the centuries to follow, large areas of Africa, America, and eventually Asia would become colonies of the Western powers. By the 19th century, the Middle Kingdom—which during Zheng He's time had surpassed the European nations in wealth, skill, sophistication, and technology—lagged far behind the West technologically and militarily, suffering a series of humiliating defeats and being forced to sign disadvantageous treaties in the process.

Yet while his epic voyages did not result in the establishment of far-flung Chinese colonies or lead to long-term advantage for China, Zheng He's accomplishments should not be minimized. (It is notable that, unlike the Europeans, China made no attempt to conquer and colonize the nations Zheng He visited, even though it was much stronger than these nations.) What Zheng He did achieve for China was equal trade relations and cultural and economic exchanges with many nations. More important, his voyages opened wide the gate of Chinese immigration to Southeast Asia. The Chinese immigrants brought advanced science and technology to this area and promoted its economic development. As a result, traditional Chinese culture was spread throughout Southeast Asia.

Today, Zheng He is well remembered in Southeast Asia, where numerous temples built in his name still attract thousands of worshipers. Many streets and towns were named after this extraordinary Chinese explorer and diplomat, and stories are still told of "the Eunuch of Three Gems" and the once great fleet that he commanded.

A man carves up a giant mushroom outside an herbal medicine shop in Hong Kong. Herbal remedies have always been a crucial component of traditional Chinese medicine, and the 16th-century doctor Li Shizhen is famous for compiling a monumental reference book on the subject.

# China's Greatest Pharmacologist

In recent years, such healing practices as herbal medicine, acupuncture, and *qigong* (*ch'i kung*) have attracted a good deal of attention among health-conscious Westerners, who are likely to group these practices into the category "alternative medicine." For the Chinese, however, they are by no means "alternative." In fact, they have been the mainstream medical practices in China for many centuries.

## Traditional Chinese Medicine

Traditional Chinese medicine, with a history of more than 2,000 years, has a unique system of diagnosis and cure. Its fundamental approach is very different from that of Western medicine. In Western medicine the focus is primarily on anatomy and biochemistry: the body is essentially understood as a machine composed of many discrete parts—cells,

tissues, organs, and structures—that work together through various physiological processes. When illness or disease arises, the part or process that is broken or not functioning properly must be identified and repaired to restore health  Traditional Chinese medicine, by contrast, not only bases its understanding of the human body on a holistic idea of the universe but also regards the human body as an integral part of the universe. The Chinese universe is based on the yin and yang dualism, which defines everything in terms of two opposite forces. Yin is the feminine, static, and dark element, represented by women, water, and the night; yang is the masculine, active, and bright element, represented by men, fire, and the day. Yin and yang depend on each other and at the same time alternate with each other to bring about balance and harmony. A typical example is the relationship of day and night: without the day there would be no night, and night and day alternate to produce a habitable world. Similarly, the yin and yang elements in the human body have to be kept in balance for a person to stay healthy.

In Chinese medicine, the core of the human body is the "five *zang* and six *fu*." *Zang* refers to the five solid organs: the heart, lungs, liver, spleen, and kidneys. *Fu* refers to the six hollow organs: the gallbladder, stomach, small intestine, large intestine, bladder, and a functional unit called *jiao* (*chiao*) between the five solid organs. These *zang-fu* organs play a crucial role in the production, maintenance, and movement of blood and vital energy, called *qi* (*ch'i*), in the human body. The three therapies of Chinese medicine—herbal medicine, *qigong*, and acupuncture—aim to regulate various functions of the body through different approaches. While acupuncture stimulates certain areas of the external body, *qigong* tries to restore the flow of blood and the vital energy through the regulation of *qi*. Herbal medicine, on the other hand, works on the *zang-fu* organs.

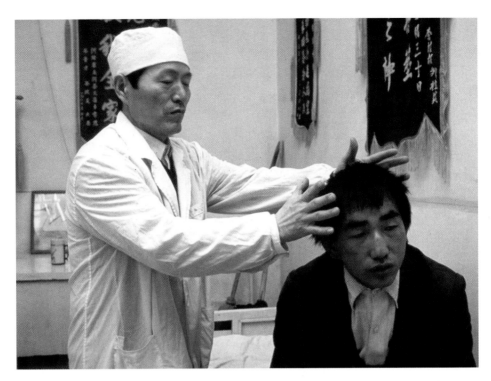

**A Chinese doctor uses *qigong* to treat a patient in a hospital. This form of Chinese folk medicine involves the concentration of vital energy on healing.**

## Chinese Herbal Medicine

At any herb store in Chinatown, one will find row upon row of wooden drawers filled with strange-looking substances (mostly dried plants) and very likely displays of ginseng roots, deer antlers, and curled snakes in big bottles of wine. Strange as they may look, these are the herbal medicines that have kept the Chinese healthy for thousands of years. About 80 percent of Chinese herbal remedies come from plants (hence the name), but animal parts and a small portion of mineral substances are also used. Since the remote past, there have been numerous stories about how the Chinese discovered the medicinal properties of various plants. The legendary founder of Chinese medicine and farming, Shennong (Shen-nung), who lived before recorded history, was said to have tasted hundreds of herbs (and to have been poisoned 70 times in one day as a result). The

**Weighing ingredients at a modern-day Chinese herb shop. In China the medicinal properties of plants were first investigated during ancient times, and over the centuries various physicians wrote works summarizing the accumulated knowledge for medical practitioners. Such authors included Li Shizhen's father, who also wrote about medical diagnostic techniques.**

Chinese have written many texts on the identification, classification, and medical qualities of various medicinal herbs. The subject of this chapter, Li Shizhen (Li Shih-chen), was a famous doctor who compiled one of these monumental works. His book *Bencao Gangmu* (*Pen Ts'ao Kang Mu*), or *The Compendium of Materia Medica* (also translated as *The Great Compendium of Herbs* or *The Great Pharmacopoeia*), was a summing-up of the pharmacological knowledge accumulated in the 2,000 years before his time. It has since been the major reference book in traditional Chinese medicine.

## A Family of Doctors

In 1518, in the middle of China's Ming dynasty (1368–1644), Li Shizhen was born into a family of doctors in a small village north of Qizhou (Ch'i-chou) in today's Hubei Province. His grandfather was a *lingyi* (*ling-i*), or "doctor on the road," who traveled from place to place to sell his services as a diagnostician and healer. Although popular with the poor people, "doctors on the road" were often grouped with astrologers and fortune-tellers and were looked down upon in Chinese society. Since ancient times, the Chinese had regarded agriculture as the foundation of the society. They disdained merchants, considering them parasites who produced nothing but lived on others, and they also downplayed the value of crafts and technology, including the practice of medicine. As a result, the medical profession had never enjoyed high status.

Li Shizhen's grandfather died before his grandson was born. According to legend, when Li Shizhen's father went to wash his hands in a nearby lake after the funeral, the water smelled of strong medicine. A fortune-teller interpreted this as a sign of the birth of a great doctor into his family. This great doctor, of course, was Li Shizhen.

Li Shizhen's father, Li Yanwen (Li Yen-wen), was a quite accomplished doctor. He had obtained a higher status than his father as a more traditional scholar-doctor. He wrote what is believed to be the first book on ginseng, as well as a few other books on the four diagnostic techniques of Chinese medicine (to look, to listen, to ask, and to feel the pulse), all of which remain influential today. When Li Shizhen was young, Li Yanwen would take him along on his trips into the mountains to collect medicinal herbs. He would also let Li Shizhen observe him while he diagnosed and prescribed medicine for patients. Thus from a very young age, Li Shizhen developed a considerable knowledge of herbs and their medicinal qualities, as well as the treatment of illnesses.

All through his boyhood, Li Shizhen was in poor health and had to rely heavily on medicine, which generated in him a personal interest in becoming a doctor. Because he was well aware of the low status of the profession, however, Li Yanwen wanted his son to follow a different path. At that time, the only way for a person outside of the imperial circles to advance himself was by taking the civil service examinations, which were mostly based on the Confucian classics. Li Shizhen devoted much of his youth to studying the Confucian classics and composing *bagu wen* (*pa ku wen*), or "eight-legged" essays (highly structured, eight-part essays required for the civil service examinations in the Ming dynasty). At 14 Li Shizhen passed the exam at the county level and became a *xiucai* (*hsiu ts'ai*), a "county graduate." However, when he moved on to the provincial level three years later, he failed three times.

Li Shizhen was never interested in becoming a traditional scholar of philosophy, law, and bureaucratic procedures. His passion was always medicine. Although he continued to study the classics for some years, he was more and more convinced that this path was not for him. At 23 he announced to his father his determination to quit the scholarly studies and become a doctor. Despite his initial reservations, Li Yanwen was supportive of this decision, for he had long noticed his son's talent in medicine. He took Li Shizhen as his apprentice, passing on to him all his clinical experience and helping him become established as a doctor.

## Years of Diligent Study

Before long, Li Shizhen became a well-known doctor in the area. Besides his medical practice, he was also very interested in medical research, especially in pharmacology. He immersed himself in his father's collection of medical books. It was said that he studied for 10 years without leaving his courtyard. While it is unlikely that a practicing doctor could actually afford to remain in his home for this long a period, the story nonetheless illustrates how devoted Shizhen was to learning.

Because Chinese medicine relies on herbs, there had been a rich herbal literature since ancient times. The first comprehensive work on pharmacology, *Shennong's Materia Medica*, appeared in the late

Han dynasty (206 B.C.–A.D. 220). It described 365 medicinal herbs and was a collection of all the discoveries relating to medicinal applications accumulated by the ancient Chinese. In the centuries that followed, various supplementary and explanatory writings based on this work appeared, some commissioned by the emperors of the Tang dynasty (618–907). In 1108, during the Song dynasty (960–1279), a famous doctor in Sichuan called Tang Shenwei compiled *The Classified Materia Medica*, which described 1,558 medicinal substances and more than 3,000 medical formulas. This was the most comprehensive book on Chinese pharmacology during Li Shizhen's time.

Li Shizhen carefully studied all of the classic medical texts. Although he admired the splendid work his forerunners had done, he also found many mistakes they had made in theory and observation, including conflicting information, wrong classification of herbs, and omission of important details. He felt an obligation to correct these mistakes.

In addition, during the 400 years since *The Classified Materia Medica*, new technological and scientific knowledge had greatly advanced the understanding and application of medicinal substances. With

**To learn more about the medicinal properties of herbs, Li Shizhen spent years exploring the mountains and fields of China.**

the expansion of China's physical territories and the development of remote areas, many new medicinal substances had been discovered. The seven grand voyages made by Zheng He to Southeast Asia, the Indian Ocean, and East Africa during the early Ming dynasty had also brought back many foreign medicines. These new developments remained to be recorded.

Li Shizhen also recognized another limitation of the classic medical texts, most of which had been written by scholar-doctors serving in the imperial courts. These doctors looked down upon practitioners like Li Shizhen's grandfather and were biased against the medical formulas such practitioners used. Working among the people, Li Shizhen knew very well that many of these medical formulas were quite effective.

All of these considerations convinced Li Shizhen to compile another book on Chinese pharmacology based on *The Classified Materia Medica*. In this new book, which was to be called *Bencao Gangmu* (*The Compendium of Materia Medica*), he would incorporate all the new medicinal discoveries and developments since Tang Shenwei's time and provide a more detailed classification of medicinal substances.

Li Shizhen kept up his diligent study for this grand project. Fully aware that pharmacology—like any other scientific discipline—was not an isolated field, he read extensively in literature, philosophy, history, geography, astronomy, botany, and chemistry, from which he gained knowledge that would later benefit his writing. Although he disliked the rich, Li Shizhen was forced to cultivate contacts with them to pursue his studies, for at the time only wealthy people had large collections of books.

Eventually, in 1558, the governor of Hubei recommended Li Shizhen to the Imperial Medical Academy for the post of court doctor. While serving in that capacity in Beijing, the Ming capital, Li Shizhen petitioned the court several times for official support for the compilation of *Bencao Gangmu*. None of these petitions met with success. After only a year's service, he left this official post on the excuse of poor health. This short stay, however, had provided Li Shizhen with a distinct advantage, for he had been able to study many rare medical texts in the imperial libraries and had learned about many foreign medicinal substances.

After returning to practice in his native town, Li Shizhen continued his research for *Bencao Gangmu*. When he started writing the book, however, he quickly realized that he didn't have a clear idea of the habitat, conditions for growth, or appearance of many of the medicinal herbs in the wild. It didn't take him long to recognize that the solution to this problem lay not in the many hundreds of books he had studied, but in nature itself. He had to go out to the mountains and fields to make direct observations and verify the information found in the books. Thus Li Shizhen started his many years of extensive travel across Hubei, Hunan (Hu-nan), Jiangxi (Chiang-hsi), Jiangsu (Chiang-su), and Anhui (An-hui). In the process he made friends with ordinary people such as farmers, fishermen, woodcutters, and hunters, and he gained from them a great deal of knowledge not available in books. Li Shizhen also took a student with him on his travels. This student, Pang Xian (P'ang Hsien), would later help him greatly with the writing of *Bencao Gangmu*.

## A Monumental Work

In 1578, after many long years spent gathering information and writing, Li Shizhen finally finished *Bencao Gangmu*—but this turned out to be but a draft. Twenty-seven years had passed since he'd first started planning for this book, but the meticulous Li Shizhen wanted the work to be perfect. Over the course of about a decade, he revised the book several times, substantially rewriting the previous version each time. Toward the end, he drafted all the members of his family and his student Pang Xian to help.

The final version was a huge work of almost 2 million words. In its 52 volumes, Li Shizhen classified a total of 1,892 medicines he had gathered or learned about into 16 categories: Water, Fire, Earth, Metals and Rocks, Herbs, Grains, Vegetables, Fruits, Wood, Clothing and Instruments, Insects, Fishes, Shells, Birds, Animals, and Materials from the Human Body. Each of these categories was subdivided into several general headings. For instance, under "Herbs" there were "Mountain Herbs," "Aromatic Herbs," "Poisonous Herbs," and several others. For each medicine, Li Shizhen included a description of its appearance, the place where it was found, the method of getting it, the manufacturing process (roasting or other ways of purification), and an analysis of its properties and effects. The majority of the 1,892 medicinal substances (nearly 1,100) were from plants; more than 440 were from animals, with an additional 275 from mineral sources. Li Shizhen also described modern chemical processes such as distillation, crystallization, and precipitation. He not only corrected the mistakes he identified in the existing medical texts, but also added 374 new medicines. In addition, he listed more than 11,000 medical formulas, the majority of which (over 8,100) were new ones he had spent his lifetime gathering from ordinary people. Li's book contained more than 1,000 illustrations of medicinal herbs, an effort unmatched by any previous scholars. Some of these illustrations were revised from old drawings in existing texts, but many were new.

*Bencao Gangmu* was not only a monumental work in Chinese pharmacology, but also a considerable contribution to botany, zoology, and mineralogy, as it detailed the variations of a great number of plants, animals, and minerals. It is reported to have helped Charles Darwin, who published *The Origin of Species* in 1859, in developing his theory of evolution. The unique classification used in *Bencao Gangmu* also came close to the modern binomial system of classification introduced by Carl Linnaeus in the 18th century.

*Bencao Gangmu*, however, was not without its limitations. The most frequent criticism concerns its enormous size, which makes it difficult to pick out the important information and also clumsy for practitioners to use. Mistakes were unavoidable in such a giant work, as is clear from the superstitious inclusion of "dirt by a widow's pillow" and "clothing of a filial son" as medicinal substances. Nonetheless, *Bencao Gangmu* marked a new height in traditional Chinese medicine, and it is considered an indispensable tool to this day.

Unfortunately, Li Shizhen didn't live to see the publication of his masterpiece, which was first published in Nanjing in 1596, three years after his death. (Of his other books, only two, both on pulse diagnosis, survive today.) After its publication, *Bencao Gangmu* quickly spread across the country and was soon regarded as the best reference work in Chinese pharmacology. In 1606 it was introduced into Japan, and later it was also translated into Latin, German, French, English, Russian, and many other languages.

Since its publication in the late 16th century, *Bencao Gangmu* has been the unrivaled text for Chinese pharmacology and one of the most quoted books in the Chinese herbal traditions. As the author of this masterpiece, Li Shizhen is unsurpassed among the major figures in traditional Chinese medicine. His image can be found in every traditional medical college in China and in many illustrated books on the history of Chinese medicine. It is generally agreed that he was the greatest naturalist of the Ming dynasty and the greatest pharmacologist in the history of traditional Chinese medicine.

Mao Zedong (1893–1976) casts his ballot in a 1953 election for local Communist leaders. As chairman of the Chinese Communist Party, Mao ruled the People's Republic of China for more than 25 years.

# Founder of the People's Republic of China

For China the 20th century was a period of enormous turmoil and momentous changes. No single figure is more emblematic of these turbulent times—indeed, no single figure did more to shape these times—than Mao Zedong (Mao Tse-tung). Mobilizing the support of China's largest group, the peasant farmers, Mao not only defeated militarily the rival Nationalist government and established the People's Republic of China, but also transformed the country from a semi-colonial feudal society into a Communist state. Nevertheless, his reputation is today decidedly mixed, for while China under his 27-year rule experienced significant progress in some respects, it also suffered through periods of humanitarian disaster and extreme social chaos, much of which was directly or indirectly attributable to Mao's policies.

## Rural Roots

Mao Zedong was born on December 26, 1893, in a village of Hunan (Hu-nan) Province in the interior of China. His father was a fairly well-to-do farmer and grain dealer. At eight, Mao was sent to the village elementary school, where he studied the Chinese classics, primarily Confucian texts, and learned to write in classical style and compose poems in the traditional way.

At the turn of the 20th century, China lagged far behind many of the world's nations in development. While the Western countries and Japan were enjoying the fruits of industrialization and an accelerating pace of technological innovation, the once powerful "Middle Kingdom" suffered from centuries of self-imposed isolation and a lingering belief that nothing "foreign" could be of value. The Confucian form of government was no longer effective, and the ruling Qing (Ch'ing) dynasty, which had been established by the Manchurian minority group in 1644, was failing. From the mid-19th century on, China had suffered a series of blows to its prestige, self-esteem, and sovereignty when various Western countries and Japan defeated China in military and political confrontations and forced the rulers of the Qing dynasty to sign one-sided treaties ceding territory and authority. Just two years after Mao's birth, Japan dealt China a crushing defeat in a war that began when China tried to prevent Korea, its last important dependency, from falling under Japanese control. As a result of its loss in the Sino-Japanese War of 1894–1895, China was forced to give Japan control of Taiwan, its largest island, which became a Japanese colony. In the years to follow, more Chinese lands were yielded to foreign powers.

In the face of these setbacks, many Chinese intellectuals began actively promoting ways their country could catch up with the rest of the world. Some advocated the adoption of Western technology and institutions. Many believed that the moribund Qing dynasty—

and even the entire dynastic system—would have to be replaced. Mao was soon to join a revolution that would eventually create a whole new China.

After graduating from the village school, Mao worked in his father's fields for three years, but he was never satisfied with such a life. He didn't get along with his conventional father, who had already mapped out a future for him in the family grain business. At 15, Mao left home for Changsha (Ch'ang-sha), the capital city of Hunan, to pursue further study. It was there that he came into contact with new ideas from the West advocated by political and cultural leaders such as Liang Qichao (Liang Ch'i-ch'ao) and Sun Yat-sen.

On October 10, 1911, revolution broke out in Wuchang (Wu-ch'ang) and soon spread to many cities of China, including Changsha. The Qing dynasty quickly collapsed, and in early 1912 the Republic of China was established, with Sun Yat-sen as its provisional president. However, a military leader named Yuan Shikai soon hijacked the republican movement. After shunting Sun Yat-sen aside and declaring himself China's president, he attempted to found his own dynasty before finally being forced from power in 1916. Lacking a strong central government, China soon descended into a period of warlordism, during which most of China's territory fell under the control of various regional warlords, who fought one another for supremacy.

During this time, Mao enlisted in the republican army as a soldier, serving for half a year and experiencing the revolution on a personal level. But he soon returned to school to continue his studies. In 1918 he graduated from Hunan First Normal School and went to Beijing University, the country's foremost intellectual center, where he worked as an assistant librarian. Although he stayed on the job for only six months, this proved to be a crucial period in his intellectual development: it was at Beijing University that he came to know Communist leaders such as Li Dazhao (Li Ta-chao), the university librarian, and Chen Duxiu (Ch'en Tu-hsiu) and became drawn to their ideas. He read and studied Marxism and became convinced that it should be the philosophical basis of the Chinese revolution and would save China from poverty and backwardness. In May 1919, when the Paris Peace Conference—convened to work out peace treaties after World War I—decided to hand over former German concessions in China's Shandong (Shan-tung) Province to Japan instead of returning them to China, a massive student demonstration broke out in Beijing. Mao wrote in an editorial: "The world is ours, the nation is ours, society is ours. If we do not speak, who will speak? If we do not act, who will act?"

Mao returned to Hunan the next year. There he married his first wife, Yang Kaihui (Yang K'ai-hui), who later bore him two sons. In 1921 he became one of the dozen men who met in Shanghai to establish the Chinese Communist Party (CCP). The following year, the CCP entered into an alliance with the Kuomintang, or Nationalist Party, which had been founded by Sun Yat-sen in order to carry the republican revolution forward. The Nationalists and Communists would, from 1923 to 1927, work together in an attempt to end the civil war between the warlords and unify the country. During this time, Mao went back to Hunan and witnessed several peasant uprisings. He became aware of the revolutionary potential of the peasants, who made up 90 percent of China's population, and was convinced that the peasantry would be the leading force in the triumph of communism in China. Later he headed the important Peasant Movement Training Institute in Guangdong (Kuang-tung), which offered peasants basic education and trained them in Marxism.

## Struggle for Power

When Sun Yat-sen died in 1925, Chiang Kai-shek became the leader of the Nationalist Party, which ultimately proved an unfortunate turn for the CCP. In 1927, after a joint Nationalist-Communist military campaign against the warlords had won some important victories, Chiang turned against his erstwhile allies. He ordered Communists rounded up and shot, and thousands were killed. Mao escaped the massacre, fleeing to the border of Hunan and Jiangxi (Chiang-hsi), where he established a Communist base. This marked the beginning of his 22-year career in rural China, during which he would gain broad-based support among the people and learn key lessons that ultimately led to victory for the Communists in China.

When joined by the men brought to his base by Zhu De (Chu Teh), a former Nationalist disillusioned with Chiang Kai-shek, Mao formed the first Communist military force, called the Red Army. Although he didn't have much formal military training, Mao developed effective guerrilla warfare tactics. While Chiang strove to eliminate the Communists in big cities, the Red Army thrived in the mountains. But Mao suffered a personal loss—his wife, Yang Kaihui, was captured and executed by Chiang in 1930.

In 1934 Chiang's large and well-equipped army began a series of major military attacks—which the Nationalists referred to as "bandit extermination"—on the CCP's rural bases. Facing encirclement and annihilation, Mao had to move his forces out of the Hunan-Jiangxi area. In October of 1934 the Red Army

General Chiang Kai-shek (right, with binoculars) and other Chinese Nationalist officers examine a map while planning a military campaign. As leader of the Nationalists, Chiang was Mao's greatest rival for control of China.

started a long and dangerous fighting retreat across the mountainous areas of Yunnan, Guizhou (Kuei-chou), and Sichuan. The Long March, as the epic journey would later be called, covered more than 6,000 miles and lasted a full year. By the time Mao finally led the remnants of his force to the safety of Yan'an (Yen-an), a remote area in northern Shaanxi Province, Nationalist attacks and the harsh environment had claimed about four of every five Red Army troops who had begun the journey. But the yearlong trek would be a critical turning point in the history of China and the life of Mao Zedong: not only had the CCP survived, but Mao's leadership of the Communists had been cemented, and he was made chairman of the CCP.

Having thwarted Chiang Kai-shek's plan for "bandit extermination," Mao also emerged as a leader of national prominence. Many revolutionists who were disgusted with Chiang's Nationalist government went to Yan'an to join the Red Army, which was soon reorganized and grew rapidly with the addition of the new recruits. During this time, Mao redistributed land in the Yan'an area to peasants. He transformed his army into a force of peasant soldiers who, when not fighting, farmed to ensure self-sufficiency.

There were also changes in Mao's personal life. He divorced his second wife, He Zizhen (Ho Tzu-chen), who had gone through the Long March with him but had developed mental illness, and married again. Mao's third wife was a famous movie actress, Lan Ping, who was later called Jiang Qing (Chiang Ch'ing). She would play an important role in the last years of Mao's political career.

In July 1937 Japan launched a full-scale invasion of China. (Earlier the Japanese had conquered Manchuria, in northeastern China, and set up a puppet government there.) Faced with this grave threat, Chiang Kai-shek was forced into a second alliance with the Communists. In eight years of fighting against the Japanese, however, there was little significant cooperation between the CCP and the Nationalists. While the Communists formed small units and waged a guerrilla war against the enemy in the vast countryside, Chiang withdrew to remote Chongqing, in China's interior. During World War II the Allies designated Chiang as their supreme commander in the China theater, and he received significant military aid from the United States and the Soviet Union. Nevertheless, he largely avoided major engagements with the Japanese.

By the time Japan surrendered in 1945, bringing both World War II and China's war with Japan to an end, Mao had won the support of the peasants, and Communist base areas had been established throughout much of the eastern part of the country. Soon the uneasy alliance between the Nationalists and the CCP broke down, and

**Mao speaks at a Communist rally in the late 1930s, encouraging resistance to the Japanese, who had invaded China in 1937.**

civil war erupted in October 1945 when Chiang ordered his forces to attack the Communists. The better-equipped and more numerous Nationalist troops controlled the cities, but Mao controlled the countryside, and his mastery of guerrilla tactics eventually wore down Chiang's army. In less than five years the Communists had completely defeated the Nationalists, and Chiang and several hundred thousand of his supporters were forced to flee to Taiwan.

## At the Head of the People's Republic of China

On October 1, 1949, at Tiananmen Square in Beijing, Mao proclaimed the establishment of the People's Republic of China (PRC).

**U.S. Marines, encircled by Chinese troops, attempt to advance behind an aerial attack during the Battle of Chosin Reservoir, December 1950. China's entry into the Korean War prevented U.S. and United Nations forces from achieving victory in that conflict—but came at a high cost.**

China was once again unified, and this time under a Communist leadership. Mao, as chairman, held the top post.

Although he had defeated the Nationalists with the strategy of "encircling the cities from the countryside," Mao realized that to build the nation, the cities had to lead and guide the countryside. He visited the Soviet Union for eight weeks in late 1949 and signed a treaty with Soviet leader Joseph Stalin, by which the PRC gained economic aid in return for Soviet economic and military privileges in China.

Mao had little chance to focus on domestic economic development, however. In June 1950 the Korean War broke out when Communist North Korea invaded U.S.-supported South Korea. The United States rushed troops to the Korean Peninsula to prevent the South from being overrun, and after the United Nations Security Council condemned the North Korean aggression, various U.N. member states contributed soldiers to the conflict as well. (The U.N. forces were under the overall command of the United States.) By the end of the year, the U.N. forces had pushed the North Koreans almost to the Yalu River, which forms the China-Korea border. At that point, China entered the conflict as Mao sent about half a million Chinese soldiers streaming across the border to fight in support of Communist North Korea. The initial Chinese onslaught overwhelmed the U.N. forces, but after a long retreat they counterattacked and pushed the Chinese back to the 38th parallel, the original dividing line between North and South Korea. For the next two years, the two sides fought to a bloody standstill. What the Chinese army lacked in advanced weapons, it made up for in numbers, and by the time an armistice was signed in July 1953, at least 150,000 Chinese soldiers had been killed. One of them was Mao's eldest son, Mao Anying, who was generally believed to be Mao's heir.

After the war, Mao's focus again turned to economic matters. Adopting the Soviet model of centralized economic planning,

China created its First Five-Year Plan (1953–1957), whose goals were met by 1956. In the countryside, land was taken from wealthy landowners and redistributed among the peasants, who had long formed a serf-like class, toiling on the estates of their overlords under an arrangement that resembled the feudalism of medieval Europe. China seemed well on its way to economic development and the establishment of a more equitable, socialist society.

But then Mao launched a campaign to win over China's intellectuals, many of whom had suffered harassment and mistreatment because of their stated or supposed opposition to communism. Dubbed the Hundred Flowers Movement, this new campaign would, Mao insisted, permit freedom of expression—indeed, the chairman actually solicited criticism of the Communist Party. But when students, professors, writers, and other intellectuals took Mao at his word and unleashed a torrent of criticism against the Party and its leaders and policies, Mao quickly staunched the free flow of ideas. He also retaliated against those who had expressed their criticism. Tens of thousands were sent to the remote countryside to perform forced labor and undergo "ideological reform." For the rest of his life, Mao would distrust the educated elite.

In 1957, on the heels of the abortive Hundred Flowers Movement, Mao launched another nationwide campaign. This one would be in the

This 1957 poster shows views of life in China, including images of a manufacturing plant, a map of industrial facilities, and charts showing economic growth. Mao's Great Leap Forward was an ambitious plan for China to catch up economically with industrialized nations like the United States and Great Britain.

economic rather than the political realm, but its consequences were similarly disastrous. The Great Leap Forward was conceived as a crash program by which China would catch up with the world's leading economic powers, Great Britain and the United States, through the sheer force of its people's will and without any foreign aid (relations with the Soviet Union had by this time begun to sour). In the industrial realm, Mao decided that China could become a major steel producer if its citizens set up homemade furnaces in their backyards. But much of the steel produced in these backyard furnaces was unusable—and in many cases people had resorted to melting down finished goods such as pots and pans in order to meet the arbitrary production goals, which yielded no real economic benefit. In the countryside, peasants were organized into large, self-sufficient communes, where they worked together in the fields and rural factories, ate together in mess halls, and lived a communal life. For a variety of reasons—including a drought, the removal of personal incentives to work hard, and the incompetence and dishonesty of Party members who managed the communes—agricultural production plummeted. Yet ambitious commune managers claimed record crop yields, and when they delivered grain to the central government from their imaginary surpluses, the people living on the communes did not have enough to eat. A famine of unprecedented proportions ensued: between 1959 and 1961, as many as 30 million Chinese died of starvation.

After the Hundred Flowers debacle and the catastrophic results of the Great Leap Forward, Mao's power in the Communist Party waned, and he was even forced to step down as chairman for a while. During this time, more pragmatic Party leaders emerged. These leaders sought to help China recover by de-emphasizing political ideology and embracing practical strategies for economic development. Although he was temporarily relegated to the sidelines, Mao never admitted his mistakes in any of the ill-advised movements he had initiated. Instead, he blamed the intellectuals for failing him and the Chinese people for not being ready for the Great Leap Forward. In any case, he strongly believed that struggle itself was more important than actual results. In 1962, in response to the criticism he was facing, he issued the call "Never forget the class struggle!" This highlighted Mao's continued adherence to Communist doctrine. Over the next three years, he started a nationwide Socialist Education Movement, through which he successfully eliminated opponents in the Party leadership. By the middle of the decade, Mao would solidify his position with another major shake-up of Chinese society.

## The Cultural Revolution

As he grew older, Mao became more and more radical. He believed that many Party members had betrayed Communist doctrines; he also suspected that China's educated people supported more of the old ways than the new ways brought about by the Communist revolution. To purify the CCP of these influences, he launched yet another mass movement: the Cultural Revolution.

By the mid-1960s, some 300 million Chinese were in their teens and twenties, and Mao now appealed directly to these youthful supporters. He officially designated them the "Red Guards," as their role was to guard the Communist revolution (the color red is associated with communism) and its leader, Chairman Mao. In 1966, in eight massive rallies organized by his radical supporters, including his wife, Jiang Qing, and Lin Biao (Lin Piao), Mao appeared in person to greet hundreds of thousands of Red Guards from across the country, who spent hours shouting slogans and singing the chairman's praises. Mao charged his followers to fight feudalism and capitalism, and the Red Guards fervently embraced the spirit of his famous saying "To rebel is justified!" They ravaged the whole country in an effort to eliminate anything "old"—in the process destroying a great deal of China's cultural heritage. They persecuted and killed numerous Chinese citizens, many of them government and Party officials or intellectuals. These victims were said to be "counter-revolutionaries" or "capitalist roaders." Although Mao called off the Red Guards in 1968 when it was clear that they had gotten out of control, the turmoil they caused did not really end until Mao's death.

The Cultural Revolution (1966–1976), now referred to by the Chinese as "the Ten Years of Calamity," marked perhaps the darkest period in the history of the People's Republic of China. Largely because of his devotion to the idea of constant class struggle, Mao plunged his nation into sheer madness. Family members turned against one another; friends denounced friends; factory managers were removed by workers for putting "technical expertise" above Communist ideology; professors and teachers were humiliated by their students and banished to the countryside to perform menial labor, effectively shutting down China's educational system for a decade. And countless accused enemies of the revolution, including Party members, government officials, and others, were subject to constant physical and mental abuse.

**A group of Chinese children in uniform read from Chairman Mao's Little Red Book, circa 1968. The decade-long Cultural Revolution, which lasted until Mao's death in 1976, was a disastrous period in the history of the People's Republic of China.**

The Cultural Revolution was also a period when the glorification of Mao reached its highest point. Everywhere people praised the chairman in songs and dances. His sayings were compiled into what was called the "Little Red Book," which was carried and quoted by virtually everybody on any occasion possible. His portraits were posted in every public building and every household. In such an atmosphere of virtual deification of Mao, any slight disrespect for him, be it intentional or unintentional, would result in severe consequences such as imprisonment or even death.

Soon after Mao's death on September 9, 1976, more than 30 radical CCP leaders who were responsible for championing the Cultural Revolution, including the infamous "Gang of Four" headed by his wife, Jiang Qing, were arrested and removed from their positions by the moderate Party faction led by Hua Guofeng (Hua Kuo-feng), then the chairman of the country, and Deng Xiaoping (Teng Hsiao-p'ing), who was soon to become China's leader. The Gang of Four and other radicals were charged with forging Mao's orders and starting the Cultural Revolution and were sentenced to imprisonment. Gradually, the social and political turmoil in China subsided, and under the leadership of Deng Xiaoping and his successors, who charted a different course from that of Mao, China has enjoyed steady economic growth and begun to emerge as a new world power.

## Mao's Legacy

After his death, Mao's body was embalmed and placed in a memorial hall in Beijing for public view. The official Chinese assessment of Mao, defined by the CCP in 1981, is that his leadership was basically correct before the year 1957, while his two major programs after that, the Great Leap Forward and the Cultural Revolution, were ill planned and led to disastrous consequences. Mao was credited with organizing the Chinese into a successful revolutionary movement and transforming an impoverished and war-battered China into one of the major powers of the world. His overall contributions to China were said to outweigh the damage he caused.

Despite the mistakes he made in his later years, which resulted in the death of millions, Mao is today still well respected by most ordinary Chinese. Every day, thousands of people walk through his memorial hall for a look at his body in its crystal coffin. An enormous portrait of the chairman still overlooks Tiananmen Square

After Mao's death, his widow, Jiang Qing, and other members of the infamous Gang of Four were arrested. They were tried publicly in Beijing for their role in the Cultural Revolution, effectively ending Mao's last revolutionary experiment.

at the heart of Beijing, the capital of China. His home in Hunan and his headquarters in Yan'an have been made into museums.

While the Chinese no longer revere Mao as a demigod, by and large he is still viewed as a remarkable statesman, whose innovative thought and firm leadership guided China's Communist revolution to success and restored Chinese pride and sovereignty. His personal charm is also well recognized. Besides his political career, Mao was also fairly accomplished in traditional Chinese poetry and calligraphy. Many of his poems, famed for the literary talent they demonstrate, also well reflect the vigor and power of this extraordinary man.

# Chronology

**771 B.C.** The Zhou king is overthrown by barbarian tribes, and his successor is forced to abandon Xi'an, the capital, and flee eastward; this marks the end of the Western Zhou period.

**770–476 B.C.** The Spring and Autumn period: while the Zhou dynasty, from its new capital of Luoyang, continues to rule China in theory, actual power devolves to the rulers of the many competing city-states.

**551 B.C.** Confucius (Kongzi), who will become a famous sage, is born in the state of Lu.

**497–484 B.C.** Confucius travels among feudal states.

**479 B.C.** Confucius dies.

**475–221 B.C.** The Warring States period: a handful of powerful states fight one another for supremacy.

**259 B.C.** The future Emperor Qin Shihuang is born Yingzheng in the state of Qin.

**247 B.C.** Yingzheng becomes king of Qin at age 13.

**221 B.C.** The Qin state conquers its last remaining rival; Qin Shihuang establishes China's first unified empire, begins a dynasty that he hopes will last 10,000 generations.

**210 B.C.** Qin Shihuang dies while on an inspection tour of his empire.

**206 B.C.** The Qin dynasty is overthrown by a popular revolt, and the Han dynasty is established.

**A.D. 624** Wu Zetian is born during the early Tang dynasty to a noble mother and a prosperous merchant father; at age 14 she will become a minor concubine to the Tang emperor Taizong.

**649** After Emperor Taizong dies, Wu Zetian is sent to a temple to live out the rest of her life.

**652** The new Tang emperor, Gaozong, brings Wu Zetian back to the imperial court as his concubine.

**655** Gaozong promotes Wu Zetian to empress.

**660** Gaozong suffers a severe stroke, and Wu Zetian becomes virtual ruler of the Tang empire.

**683** Emperor Gaozong dies, and Wu Zetian's son takes the throne as Emperor Zhongzong; within two years, however, she deposes him.

**690** Wu Zetian gives herself the title "Holy and Divine Emperor."

**705** Wu Zetian dies.

**1036** Su Dongpo, who will become one of China's most beloved poets, is born Su Shi during the Song dynasty.

**1056–57** Su Dongpo passes the imperial civil service examinations with distinction.

**1061–65** Su Dongpo serves as an assistant magistrate in a poor county.

**1079** Charged with slandering the emperor, Su Dongpo is arrested, imprisoned, and later banished to Huangzhou, where he will live in difficult circumstances but write some of his best poetry.

**1086** Su Dongpo, restored to favor, receives a high court position.

**1094** Su Dongpo is again banished, this time to remote Huizhou.

**1101** A year after being permitted to return home, Su Dongpo dies.

**1371** The great explorer Zheng He is born to a Muslim family in Yunnan.

**1381** Ming dynasty forces mopping up the remnants of the deposed Yuan dynasty's followers capture Zheng He; he is castrated and sent to the Ming palace as a servant.

**1402** Zhu Di (Emperor Yongle), to whom Zheng He has been given as a personal servant and whom he has served capably as a military commander, wins a civil war and assumes the Ming throne.

**1405–33** On behalf of the Ming rulers, Zheng He commands seven massive seafaring expeditions of exploration and trade, traveling throughout Southeast Asia and the Indian Ocean and reaching the Persian Gulf, the Red Sea, and East Africa; he dies in 1433, on the return voyage of his last expedition.

**1518** Li Shizhen, who will become a famous doctor and expert in pharmacology, is born.

**1558** Li Shizhen receives a post as court doctor.

**1578** After decades of research and writing, Li Shizhen completes the first draft of *Bencao Gangmu* (*The Compendium of Materia Medica*), a voluminous and masterful work that describes and catalogs Chinese herbal remedies and formulas.

**1593** Li Shizhen dies.

**1596** *Bencao Gangmu* is published in Nanjing.

**1893** Mao Zedong is born in a small village in rural Hunan Province.

**1911** A revolution that begins in Wuchang soon spreads throughout China, leading to the overthrow of the Qing dynasty and the establishment of the Republic of China.

**1918** Mao graduates from the Hunan First Normal School and takes a position as assistant librarian at Beijing University, where he comes into contact with Marxist ideas.

**1921** Mao is among the dozen Marxists who meet in Shanghai and found the Chinese Communist Party (CCP).

**1923** The Nationalist Party (Kuomintang) and the CCP form an alliance to combat the warlords who emerged soon after the establishment of the Republic of China and who now control most of China.

**1927** Nationalist leader Chiang Kai-shek turns against his Communist allies, executes many CCP members; Mao escapes to the border of Hunan and Jiangxi and soon establishes a Communist base.

**1934–35** In the face of a Nationalist campaign to exterminate the Communists, Mao guides his soldiers on the Long March, which firmly establishes his leadership of the CCP.

**1937–45** During the Japanese invasion and occupation of China, the Nationalists and Communists are uneasy allies; in October, soon after the Japanese surrender, civil war breaks out between the two Chinese factions.

**1949** On October 1, Mao proclaims the establishment of the

People's Republic of China, following the final defeat of the Nationalists.

**1950–53** The Korean War—during which Chinese troops fight on the side of North Korea, opposing the U.S. and United Nations forces fighting with South Korea—takes place.

**1956** Mao initiates the Hundred Flowers Movement, a brief period during which freedom of expression is permitted in China; after intense criticism of the CCP, however, he cracks down hard on intellectuals and critics of the Party.

**1957** The Great Leap Forward, an economic program that Mao believes will help China catch up rapidly with Great Britain and the United States, begins; within five years the Great Leap Forward will have failed utterly, contributing to a famine that claims millions of Chinese lives.

**1966** Mao initiates the Cultural Revolution, which plunges China into 10 years of social turmoil.

**1976** On September 9, Mao dies.

# Glossary

**aristocrat**—a member of a ruling class or of the noble families.

**benevolence**—a tendency to do kind deeds.

**castrate**—to remove the testicles of a male.

**concession**—a special right to property or land.

**dualism**—the belief that reality is divided into two very different or opposing parts.

**elixir**—a magic substance believed to have the power of making one live forever.

**envoy**—someone who is sent as a representative from one government or organization to another.

**eunuch**—a castrated man, particularly one who performs duties in a palace.

**filial piety**—devotion to and respect for parents and family.

**hierarchical**—characteristic of a social or political structure in which individuals are classified according to their importance and have well-defined roles.

**holistic**—dealing with or treating the whole of something, with recognition of the interdependence of its parts.

**mandate**—the authority given to someone to perform an action or govern a country.

**pharmacology**—the science of drugs, including their composition, uses, and effects.

**reprimand**—to express strong official disapproval of something or someone.

**sage**—a well respected and wise person.

**sovereignty**—complete independence and self-government.

# Further Reading

Chang, Hui-Chien. *Li Shih-Chen: Great Pharmacologist of Ancient China*. Peking, China: Foreign Languages Press, 1960.

Faulkner, Anne. *Mao Zedong*. Austin, Tex.: Raintree Steck-Vaughn Publishers, 2003.

Freedman, Russell. *Confucius: The Golden Rule*. New York: Arthur A. Levine Books, 2002.

Jiang, Cheng An. *Empress of China, Wu Ze Tian*. Monterey, Calif.: Victory Press, 1998.

Levathes, Louise. *When China Ruled the Seas: The Treasure Fleet of the Dragon Throne 1405–1433*. New York: Oxford University Press, 1996.

Lin, Yutang. *The Gay Genius: The Life and Times of Su Tungpo*. Westport, Conn.: Greenwood Press, 1971.

Lindesay, William. *The Terracotta Army of the First Emperor of China*. Kowloon, Hong Kong: Odyssey Publications, 2003.

O'Connor, Jane. *The Emperor's Silent Army: Terracotta Warriors of Ancient China*. New York: Viking, 2002.

Wang, Cynthia. *Famous People of China*. Geelong West, Victoria, Australia: Word Connection, 1997.

# Internet Resources

**http://www.chinapage.com/china-rm.html**

A primary resource site for the Chinese classics, arts, history, literature, poetry, calligraphy, and paintings.

**http://asterius.com/china/**

This website gives a condensed Chinese history with chronology and highlights from each time period.

**http://www.chinapage.com/poet-e.html**

English translations of masterpieces by famous Chinese poets, including Su Dongpo, Li Bai, Du Fu, and Bai Juyi.

**http://www.chinapage.com/zhenghe.html**

A brief introduction to Zheng He and his grand voyages, with links to other relevant information.

**http://www.itmonline.org/docs/famous.htm**

This website from the Institute of Traditional Medicine in Portland, Oregon, lists famous Chinese doctors of the past, with their portraits and biographies.

**http://www.time.com/time/time100/leaders/profile/mao.html**

*Time* magazine's 100: Mao Zedong.

**Publisher's Note:** The websites listed on this page were active at the time of publication. The publisher is not responsible for websites that have changed their address or discontinued operation since the date of publication. The publisher reviews and updates the websites each time the book is reprinted.

# Index

Numbers in **bold italics** refer to captions.

# Picture Credits

Page
12: Corbis Images
14: Burstein Collection/Corbis
16: U.S. Library of Congress
18: Mary Evans Picture Library
21: Werner Forman/Art Resource, NY
22: Mary Evans Picture Library
25: Werner Forman/Art Resource, NY
28: Giraudon/Art Resource, NY
32: IMS Communications, Inc.
35: Giraudon/Art Resouce, NY
38: Snark/Art Resource, NY
39: HIP/Scala/Art Resouce, NY
42: Corbis Images
44: Nik Wheeler/Saudi Aramco
      World/PADIA
47: Mary Evans Picture Library
48: Asian Art & Archaeology,
      Inc./Corbis
51: Ng Han Guan/AFP/Getty Images
53: Lowell Georgia/Corbis
54: Erich Lessing/Art Resource, NY
57: Werner Forman/Art Resource, NY
60: Giraudon/Art Resource, NY
62: Réunion des Musées Nationaux/Art
      Resource, NY

66: Nik Wheeler/Saudi Aramco
      World/PADIA
68: Mariner's Museum, Newport News,
      Virginia
73: © OTTN Publishing
74: Keren Su/Corbis
76: S.M. Amin/Saudi Aramco
      World/PADIA
78: Richard A. Brooks/AFP/Getty
      Images
81: Forrest Anderson/Time Life
      Pictures/Getty Images
82: Francois Perri/Liaison/Getty Images
85: Nik Wheeler/Saudi Aramco
      World/PADIA
90: U.S. Library of Congress
95: U.S. Library of Congress
97: Hulton/Archive/Getty Images
98: National Archives
100: U.S. Library of Congress
103: Hulton/Archive/Getty Images
105: AFP/Getty Images

# Contributors

**YAN LIAO** is a native of China. She earned her M.A. in American Studies from Sichuan University, China. Later she studied at the University of Hawai'i and earned master's degrees in English as a Second Language and Library and Information Science. Currently Yan Liao is an assistant professor at the University of Wisconsin–Stevens Point.

**JIANWEI WANG**, a native of Shanghai, received his B.A. and M.A. in international politics from Fudan University in Shanghai and his Ph.D. in political science from the University of Michigan. He is now the Eugene Katz Letter and Science Distinguished Professor and chair of the Department of Political Science at the University of Wisconsin–Stevens Point. He is also a guest professor at Fudan University in Shanghai and Zhongshan University in Guangzhou.

Professor Wang's teaching and research interests focus on Chinese foreign policy, Sino-American relations, Sino-Japanese relations, East Asia security affairs, UN peacekeeping operations, and American foreign policy. He has published extensively in these areas. His most recent publications include *Power of the Moment: America and the World After 9/11* (Xinhua Press, 2002), which he coauthored, and *Limited Adversaries: Post-Cold War Sino-American Mutual Images* (Oxford University Press, 2000).

Wang is the recipient of numerous awards and fellowships, including grants from the MacArthur Foundation, Social Science Research Council, and Ford Foundation. He has also been a frequent commentator on U.S.-China relations, the Taiwan issue, and Chinese politics for major news outlets.